# Existential Dialogues II

## By

Daniel Chechick

Translation: Tom C. Atkins

Proofreading: Sharona Gury

Cover : Arina Albu

"Nothing is true, everything is permitted"

Friedrich Nietzsche

# Table of Contents

# Introduction

———————————

◆ ◆ ◆

Throughout life, a person may encounter many questions without having pause to watch and contemplate, to wonder what everything means for them, personally.

What did I ask for, other than gentle moments of existence in which I could devote myself to the silence within me and debate my spirit over real decisions on real issues?

For what is the common alternative?
To annihilate myself in blind devotion to the choices of the many who would dictate my way of life, though I never asked for their advice? Such a choice would be an insult.

I then thought there must be another way to live, before that predetermined script which some are so quick carve into the spirits of young people.

Harsh words of this kind have burst out of me, a defensive storm protecting me from the possible insult of being a leaf, blowing in the wind, without any hold, without any internal decision.

That is why I determined to hold an internal discourse with my spirit over all of those great questions which have always haunted my mind, without letting external voices be a determining factor.

Moreover, I sought to have a discussion with the old man I will become - to find an appropriate partner for these intimate conversations, so rare in the freezing reality.

Such quiet conversations, where thoughts come up uncensored, are at times a worthy reason to still live. To still be human.

# Chapter One:
## QUESTION MARKS

♦ ♦ ♦

How much would you like to live?

**Why does it matter?**

It matters to me! I must know.

**First you would have to ask me to clarify to you what kind of life is even worth living, for I don't take long life, in itself, to be an achievement.**

What kind of life is worth living, then?

**It seems that people find a worthy life in their embraces.**

Then, you would like to live as long as you embrace?

**Almost, but not exactly. A life worth living is one in which you can embrace question marks.**

And by negation, one can understand that a life that is not worth living is a life

in which one embraces exclamation marks, is that not so?

**I am not brave enough to opine on the life of others, but for me it would be inconceivable.**

*But, what does it even mean to embrace question marks?*

What is a small boy in a playground if not a walking question mark, investigating his world from within himself in previously unseen addiction? And he faces powerful forces which constantly embrace exclamation marks and seek to eliminate his wonder and deny him from searching, for they have already found for him. Have you known a violent absurd of that kind?

*So many exclamation marks in my soul did not come from within me! But these are the foundations of the world I have known since infancy. How can I disengage from such a powerful embrace? Who will I call on at a time of crisis?*

See in your world, see around you how many people live in a never ending embrace of exclamation marks that have become dear to them, for they have always lived in them. What a terrible distress is it for a person to ask and to hold onto doubt and helplessness.

*I would like to choose my own exclamations marks!*

You would like to choose...

*Is it too late for me to disengage from the embrace of exclamation marks?*

Do they embrace you, or are you desperate in your embrace of them?

*Good question.*

Since these exclamation marks were etched into your soul in ancient times, you can easily identify them by stripping completely bare. Your courage will then be to choose them anew, or make of them question marks which you might not even have to answer!

*Who is brave enough to become a question mark these days?*

Bravery is extremely rare, and therefore exclamation marks are so common.

*Then you seek to be brave and embrace question marks?*

As much as I can. Such would be my life, and even if I embrace one question mark, even if I embrace one exclamation mark, as long as it is mine and from within me, it would be a life worth living for me.

*It seems that it was only the first man who was immune to the projects of exclamation marks. Only he could have created his spirit in the purest way. But for you one achievement is enough.*

Self-affirmation requires a sense of modesty, for in any case one cannot realize the common exclamation marks.

*Then you will live as long as you could be a question mark?*

Definitely. It is my favorite exclamation mark.

# What exclamation marks were activated within us, and we never dared question?

# Chapter Two:
## MASK

◆ ◆ ◆

*Where are they, the people?*

Have your eyes stopped working, or have you become too proud to perceive their world?

*Why would you deride my question so? I ask again: Where are the people?*

They are always around us, can't you see? They surround us so constantly that I cannot feel my own self anymore!

*Then I ask again: Where are the people? All I see are masks.*

Does your heart wish to beguile me again?

*How is it one can no longer see the tears of disappointment in the eyes of a*

*young girl whose heart has been cleaved into two?*

They have become masters of concealment. As if to outdo the Greek sages, to the question of body and soul they added the ever changing mask, and now can no longer allow their spirit to show them crying or sad.

If they cannot express such emotions, perhaps they have adopted some Eastern wisdom that brings a man closer with himself? Could that be it? And if they were left with no opinion, did they eliminate the phenomenon of tears?

Neither one nor the other, my friend. You do not understand. They do not cry outwardly, because of the mask. But inside they are still miserable. They hide themselves from existence as if others reinforced their belief that there is power in lacking 'weakness'. For the world has become so fast that no place is left for close compassion. They are no longer interested in listening to the pains of others. That is why both sides forever portray their lives as being as wonderful as can be, and even when they ask each other for their well-being, they hint at what answer they expect.

Then they all know that they are all hiding?

True.

Is it not possible that humans have stopped giving in to crying and sadness?

Indeed.

And we will, of course, not consider the possibility that they are in a never ending state of mania?

True.

Where then does their lost soul find release?

Perhaps they hide their tears, as if they were evidence of some crime.

This is indeed a reasonable option... But another idea comes to mind: perhaps they are busy concealing their terror, and cry through the tears of others, using each other as mirrors for their own souls.

cannot but hope that this is not the case. But those made in the semblance of God cannot be immune from sadness and pain. In some way or another, therefore, they must express their emotions.

If so, those you would call *people* are few already. They may have covered their true selves, and from now on I will call them 'masked'. As babies they soon learn the social smile, and see what disaster happens after so few years. Where do they hide, those daring of emotions?

It seems that man has become a theatre of deception, and one can no longer tell apart the love of passion from the love of the soul. For they do not express their feelings well, and even if a person were ready to embrace their world, they would surely be wary that even the desire to accept them as they are is nothing but fakery.

Be careful with those bewitched thoughts!

Is it not the truth?

It is.

Then how will I penetrate through the many walls that envelop their souls?

You must reflect their absence through your authenticity, that is, to appear without a mask, if you are still able to do so.

Of course I can! I am a person.

Can you smile to the world, as in naive infatuation?

Do you give in to sadness when it meets you?

But you know my soul. I will never delude myself. Even if I'd rather smile than be sad, I'd still recognize both, as a soul that cannot always be serene but constantly moves between terror and wonder.

And what of those eternally masked? They do not know their soul at all, but are full of self-deception.

They are so masked and camouflaged that they have forgotten their original world, and are now nothing but appeasement of others. They have become accustomed to adopt characters fitting for this event or that time, hoping that by the absence of their presence they will find someone to affirm their existence.

And now, even if the most wonderful person were to meet them, the one who they longed for their whole lives, they might not be able to give in to the enchantments of loves. For it is a grand rule that as long as they have not known their very depths - their attitude towards the other will forever be shallow, eternally masking their hidden desires, to the point of disgrace, of self-contempt. How can a person fall in love with another, while he constantly despises his own soul?!

And even were he to feel love, would he still hide his world? Would he always despise his authentic Self, hidden somewhere in the depths?

Shall we consider the possibility of a miracle? Of misguided faith, which slowly turns true, that through seeing the great heart of another the many walls around his soul would slowly dissolve and he would become a person, perhaps for the first time in his existence?

What a healing perspective you contain! And I was so close to despair with all those "masked".

At times the "masked" outside are nothing but a person's so human will for inner regression... but it was nothing but a quiet longing to once again be safe and protected, as in days past when he did not yet know the depths of his soul.

I will surprise you and say that there is no higher satisaction for a person than exposure, by which he expresses the divinity in his soul, as if saying: this is my life's play, and it's your choice whether to take part or to leave - all by the power of a smile and self-intimacy, and not, God forbid, in vain, negative power.

Therefore, a person should express the extremes of his soul without concealment, as if he were human, aware of the recesses of his hidden soul, his secret desires, his forbidden passion and noble thoughts. May he would be wonderful and terrible, complete and imperfect, vulnerable and uncovered, as an intimate embrace that contains him and the other, for now he already knows that the other is near him, and that they both find their path through the treacherous rocks of the ocean of contentions. And they have but a humble wish, all they ask is to be human and authentic in their lives' play.

# Did you expose your world to the bone in the performance of your life, or have you become addicted to the mask?

# Chapter Three:
## LESSER LIGHT

◆ ◆ ◆

My soul is concerned with intricate matters, such that can no longer be held back. Since I first felt them, they began to take hold of my being, never loosening their grip, they ceaselessly stir my anxieties.

**Let your thoughts gush forward. It seems they will inevitably do so in any case.**

It seems I do not know how to overcome my existential questions. Or to put it bluntly, I do not know the purpose of my existence.

**How did you raise your conceit so high as to ask for a purpose and a reason for your existence, as if you perceived your own being to be part of some grand, impressive plan?**

Far be it. But why would you see my world as conceit? For this question has been troubling humans since the earliest days of their existence. See how they philosophize for millenia, endlessly deliberating over every decision. And everyone takes the same final path, do they not?

**What good is it for a man to ponder the reason for his existence? He is here already, and cannot kill himself.**

It is not clear how the lack of purpose scares a person more than the lack of life itself, but it seems that they are close. In any case, you escape to the other terror, the one maybe perceived as an answer to the burden of the existential question... But I will not relent! Teach me how to endure.

I cannot teach you how to endure when you ask unfitting questions. A person must remove his inclination to anthropomorphize his world. For how can you bestow purely human concepts to natural phenomena?

What do you mean?

It is easy for a person to assume that if there is a watch, then there must be a watchmaker, and that therefore if creation exists, it must have a purpose. The mistake is when a person applies the conclusions of his own creation to the boundless existence, when it is clear that a person has no influence on it. Inside this reality a person excels in wondering and exploring his own world. This brings about more human creations, but at the same time, through a terrible act of repression, the person also understands that not all existential questions have clear answers, unlike the aforementioned watchmaker, who can easily clarify the purpose of his own creation.

Cease stomping my spirit with the coldness of your thought. For you are talking to the lost spirit, while I express a human difficulty in me, and certainly in many other people around me! Isit so terrible to adopt fictions which comfort my soul? Is my bravery in adopting a lie not greater than the righteous coldness of your thought? How can you not understand this reversal?

Why then should you ask about the purpose of your existence? You have already adopted a lie that seals a search of 'truth' within you, as if you fell in love with the mask of false security, and forgot the helplessness which takes over your crass wishes!

*Do not think that this mask satisfies my spirit. Many questions in me threaten*

*to topple my world. And is that any surprise?*

Now that you recognize that you adopted a fiction, all cards fall uncontrollably. It is clear to me what your next question is. You can no more hide it from me than if I could see into your mind.

*It may be the most terrible question of all.*

Is there a greater compliment for a person than being perceived as the center of the universe, as the deluded baby perceives itself to be?

*Nothing is more wonderful.*

If you agree to that, can you leave your mind for a few meager moments, and imagine what the lesser light would say to himself, looking outwards to the universe and repressing its own thoughts, and it dares to ask bluntly: 'could the world have been created without me? Could my absence have gone completely unnoticed?'. These questions of the lesser light, they are unconsciously also the most terrible questions of a man, as he perceives his life's play to be a unique, un-repeating phenomenon. And as he questions his existence he is filled with dread that all of this could have not happened at all! Are you able to imagine a world where your entire being never existed?!

*Of course not! Please cease that talk!*

Then, it must be that these questions come not out of curiosity, but of our destructive pride, which hides from us the naive experience to live as a child in love with its own world. Such a question seeks divinity, when it is clear for all to see that a man is but a grain of sand and his life are but a small candle, but the heart's desire seeks to be a sun. Do you understand what I say?

This is the essence of a person's spirit!

*How can I be a grain of sand, accepting the burden of the kingdom of God.*

*Where will I find the humility for that?*

Look at the wonderful flowers. They are enviously colorful, and many hues of love reflect in them at any moment. They are completely exposed as if there were nothing to hide, so much so that they are willing to be plucked at any given moment, offering no resistance. But still they keep their humility. Why is that? Since flowers do not ask what is the meaning of blooming. They simply bloom. They are not concerned with tales and fictions; they are delicate and small and still more beautiful than the man who, instead of giving in to the passion of life, to the simple pleasures, is always busy with his pride, changing hues and even plays terrible tricks to disguise himself, enveloped in modesty inside the games of his mind. What is my prayer for man? All I ask is that he be human. Why is that so unfathomable, how is it that all he does is guided by his wish to reach divinity, even though he knows it is a doomed war?

*Is it possible that my friend faults me, while the same flaw exists within him, under a different guise?*

In what way?

*You have described the terrible mistake by which a person draws conclusions from the purpose of his own creations and his lowly desire, almost to the purpose of the great existence. As if he was no less important than the lesser light. And now you ask a person to be a person, as if it were obvious; where does a person find the experience to be a person? It is well known that a person is never given a chance to be himself, for he is given by others in the crucial years* in which he is shaped. And if by some miracle he manages to be a man for a few simple moments in his life, then that is his pride. However, life ends soon and fast, so that this miraculous tale should not be known to the many. Moreover, you ask a person to learn from the colorful flowers, for they grant the wish, they just bloom. Then you asked to draw conclusion from the smaller to the larger, the same mistake as comparing the watch to the universe. So frankly I ask you, my friend, how will you compare the flower  that knows nothing other than to bloom and the man, who does not even know how to be a man?

My heart trembles at your words: "the man, who does not even know how to be a man." You have shattered my thoughts to the abyss, and I can do nothing but embrace you, as the bible reads (reprove not a scorner, lest he hate thee: rebuke a wise man, and he will love thee - proverbs 8,9). And a new query immediately comes to me of man's spirit. If he cannot neutralize the influence of others' fictions on him, then certainly he would tend towards the heavens, towards faith and escape, rather than enjoy the simple things in life. His dispositions are therefore not surprising, as if he chose his endless inner wars, those who do not leave him the simple pleasure and demand that he commits to the fictions of his imagination, which confirm his existence and comfort his agonizing questions. And I no longer know whether a man can even be a man.

It seems that forming such intimate thoughts seeks to express a different, perhaps even more painful thought. For in other times, millenia past, a person was closer to himself and knew himself so much that he could give in to these flowers and accept their world into him as a nirvana-filled inspiration. While now, modern socialization has overcome him from infancy, and his spirit is full *of fictions from the crib. And as he cannot let go of these, he would rather adopt many other imaginations over the most terrible choice, the so hidden option of understanding that he never had the chance to really know himself.*

Then his aspiration towards divinity is nothing but an attempt to escape this difficult insight.

*And what has been decided on our matter?*

What are you aiming at?

*What is it that pulls me towards fiction and you towards relentless examination?*

It seems that in their roots, our spirits are close. But they are directed to different ends. A struggle between my passion for the truth and my knowledge that the most solid truth is the lack of truth. Or at least, my human inability to perceive or understand it. The very process of examination and purification brings a smile to my world, while you operate on the other end: you are aware that there is no truth, but you hold on to 'fictions of truth' and can bring a smile to your own world, as if through a magic trick I cannot understand.

*As long as we both bring a smile to our world, it seems that we have found truth, purpose and meaning.*

# What is your answer to the question of meaning?

# Chapter Four:
## GENTLE NOTES

◆ ◆ ◆

Your imagination must still hold that time I was all alone, when I crudely eliminated any ability to give love to that wonderful woman I loved so much, does it not?

**Indeed, I remember it all. You were alone in the world.**

I was so lonely, I thought my loneliness was deeper than before I was born.

**But why do you think far to those days?**

For in those days it seemed that my world became dark shades, as if I stopped noticing the beauty of the fall and all of existence around me. And I thought that I could never again love like that, for that joining of spirits was as rare in existence as a rainbow, which will always be unique in the eyes of lovers. But by looking at my world today, I learned to notice the soul slowly healing, as if it learned to appreciate its existence to its fullest.

**And how was your spirit healed if your love was severed?**

Wait a while with insights regarding my healing. My spirit still seeks to describe my feelings from that time. For I have almost fallen to the deep sadness of losing my closest friend, my trusted confidant, my soul mate - the one who for many years persisted in accepting the terror, and the wonder, in me... and I am well aware of how rare this acceptance is in our world.

**And not only that, but the person to whom you could fully express your love, the one whose soul, in the words of the hymn – "pines for your love".**

But see what I recently thought. My spirit was almost burned by my clear loss. But magical insights have fallen like smiling raindrops on my cheeks, allowing me to take a close look at my noble experiences. At first I thought I should raise my spirits, for the wonderful shared world I took part in for long years serves as confirmation that one can pain over worthy things.

In other words - it is acceptable for the heart to ache when you loved in the full sense of the word. Some seperate after hard, bad years, as if finally managing to break loose, but at the same time crying for not doing so earlier. But you have loved all that time, were excited no end. You were addicted, as if your beloved were a drug.

And moreover, I understood another great enchantment, that my spirit was wholly changed during that time. So it may be that some loves are right for a person in certain times, but should not chain him forever.

A person's life is dynamic, his wishes change constantly, and what he needs at this time he will not necessarily need at other times. Only the brave can understand such an insight, for hearts are broken after the fact.

And I had another thought, that when I appreciate my life to its fullest, certainly my heart will be able to contain another wonderful love of another spirit, and I could lose myself in it as a wonderful sob hides in the sensitivity of the piano's notes.

And after all those thoughts, another obscure question remains, of how the lover draws away from the object of his love.

So terrible is your question, it shatters any attempt of healing in me.

Is it possible that you did not love at all?

Of course I loved! I loved her more than I loved myself.

Why, then?

Should I inwardly think that there is no sufficient reason for me to love her endlessly?

My experience taught me that at times love changes its hues, as if it lost its primacy.

Perhaps my spirit seeks to reach the eternal fire. As if I am no longer modest enough for the smaller bliss.

This kind of life lessons are not learned quickly.

Inwardly I thought how to decide in such a complex topic. Her whole world, whose emotional intensity I could not imagine is rooted in me.

Terror resides when repression is eliminated, and by that the choice to contend is forced - as an axiom that can no longer be ignored. And when certainty leads you, you cannot do otherwise.

Is it possible that she had thought so even before I did, but hid it from me as if deciding that our love and our shared world were more important than anything to her?

It is possible.

Be that as it may. Longings force endless memories of the world I had on my consciousness, and the wisdom of great appreciation, and a smiling hope that my world and hers will still enchant a man and a woman on their path, and my heart still holds grace for her, as if to breath her youthful spirit, my first love, the most wonderful one I could have asked for.

It is beautiful that such is the case. I am full of hope that she shares that perspective, with the obvious heart ache in it.

And another thing I found in me after a period of observation, that not only did I decide to sever myself from her world, but I also beat the depth of my soul and knew the pains of the heart, that cannot lay down their red-hot knives.

And now you expressed the most painful thoughts of love, as an existential dread, that every man can be replaced.

And is that not true?

Brazenly true, and a good thing, too.

*Why for?*

For otherwise we could definitely not live even one more day.

*But we are human, and we know how far thoughts of loneliness can take us.*

But still, internally you know that it was not a substitute, for each love represents a rainbow of emotions in colors unique to it alone, as a new creation that is unlike anything else in your existence.

*Like a melody that was never before heard?*

Yes, an instrument that was not yet made - one tuned only to your delicate ears. And you should know that in old age I could express more sounds, as if being excited anew after a period of real mourning, during which I was brave enough to look inside myself without concealment, and confess my deep sins, as well as our magical moments.

*After a deep introspection, that took quite a while, I could feel in me emotional availability to gentle notes of the spirit which I could let ring. And from this transcendence, which is nothing short of a miracle, I could also ask that she allows herself to make a beautiful sound which was unique to her alone.*

You had a magical melody.

*And in your world?*

Are you in doubt?

*Your ears are sensitive to the most gentle of sounds.*

It seems that without a proper struggle which lasted for a long time, I could have, God forbid, sentenced myself to draw inward, in a guise of drawing away from others. But when the flames of existence singed the bedrock of my world I could slowly watch new and colorful flowers open in me, able to express emotional availability to a brave new world, and without contradicting the memories of the spirit from which they forever took root.

# What does break up mean for us?

# Chapter Five:
## ON LOVE

◆ ◆ ◆

How can a person live their whole life and never experience close love?

*Do you really imagine that there are such people?*

There is humanity in me, and my eyes still see the struggling man, the one who tries to hide his lonely world. For he walks inside of us, as if trying to eliminate his most hidden secret. But he always stands out, as people are so bewitched that they fix their attention on the misfits of existence, on those who make them appreciate their own world. And they simply feel pity towards them.

*Is it possible that this thought can be repressed to such a degree? Is that not*

*the greatest loss in the play of life?*

What should people do, if this is their experience? This is their reality and they must deal with it, and perhaps push it completely away, giving such excuses or others. For deep inside, they know that they would not be able to bear such a terror.

*Could it be that such people experienced their loves through the stories of*

*others, and now project themselves through their imaginary illusions,* whenever in the depths of their heart they fall in love with strangers who will never know their feelings?

We know that an infinite gap separates illusion and thought from active experience. A man becomes his own grand illusionist in his love stories, but nothing compares to the look of love in her eyes or her caress on my flesh, as shivers running down my embraced heart.

It is like the miracle that happens to those who were blind since birth, and by virtue of a brilliant operation saw their world for the first time. For them, it is an explosion of emotions similar to the heart overflowing with love.

Moreover, I know that in distant lands loneliness is so terrible, that they invented a hugs-by-delivery services. Could you believe it? They are so forlorn, that they require the close caress even though they know that fundamentally it is empty. This profession has become so commonplace among them.

How demeaning!

To what other lengths can you go?

At times I look at the faces of strangers, and I have a growing feeling that I could have loved them. It suddenly seems that man and dog grew from the same seed. Both have hearts that never cease to give and seek love, as if it were the purpose of their existence. But man is so removed from that reality. Imagine how a dog wags its tail, it cannot but be excited by his many encounters. And then think of the unloved man, who no one has figuratively wagged its eyes towards. As if he were walking in the street and even the most gentle dogs forgot his existence and abandoned his stroking hand.

**Perish that thought! So much humanity exists in the soul of dogs, they know the loneliness of people and constantly bring a smile to their world. And as complicated as a man's life is - still his spirit is excited and melts in the face of a dog's unquestioning love, as if he were embraced by it and, in that, his worth was affirmed, as if sharing the sensitivity of the great Dostoyevsky who said that hell is the suffering of being unable to love.**

And at a second glance, I imagine a reality in which the emotions of others were clear to us, as if they could not hide them, just as dogs cannot. See yourself walking the streets, and they uncontrollably react to you with a smile that uncovers their desire to come in and sniff, or in other words - to simply embrace you and say hello, to give you the feeling that you are worthy, that your existence intrigues and enchants them.

**Perhaps everything can be concluded in man's so clear need to feel worthy?**

What can be a greater confirmation of his worth to a person than the love of others? This is always perceived as the greatest compliment in existence. And without feeling that they touched the highest peak, they must continue at all times to desire, as if addicted to the unattainable, and are left an empty vessel to their unending thoughts. And moreover, their thoughts question their self-love, that which should seemingly fill the void. And at the same time, the person asks to understand how one who has loved himself - so rare in the world - has yet to project to others their love to him, as if he asked for a magical equation that draws love to those who love themselves. And after concluding these *thoughts they become even more secluded in themselves, for they cannot ignore*

*their clear sadness even if they wanted to disappear.*

How can a man stop aspiring for love? See, even divinity in its various forms demands unending love, desperate as it is for the tears and attention of humans. It has found for them so many ways to love, and at times they have risked their lives under the excuse of the love of God, but this is an embrionic love, so virginal and primal that even those who receive it seek no dowery or recognition, exactly because God is so unattainable.

*But this is existential love, from the depth of the heart. There is nothing similar*

*to it in man's reality. These are forms that cannot exist but between mortal*

*man and the God in his thought. As I delve deeper I am filled with the wonder*

*that the unloved man may have known in the souls of others the same feelings,*

*and through an almost motherly desire have invented for them a peaceful way*

*to love. For it is the lack of their love in their world that he brazenly made into*

*an addiction for the unknown, and by that they filled their hearts with his*

*boundless love. Could you imagine such wisdom? Is that not the greatest cure*

*for humanity?*

Such a wonderful loving spell! For wisdom comes from knowing solace in complete love directed into a man's heart with no effort. For he can hardly live in the hearts of his friends, but he continues to perceive in his spirit that his maker loves him more than anything, and even takes care to plan for him life missions and pour meanings into the play of his life. And this is wonderful for the loved man. For he gains from men and even from the almighty, and if I skip in thought to the most miserable, the sick and abandoned, the dying, the wretched, the despised - then won't God's unquestioned love be a perfect and wonderous solace? I was almost convinced to believe this tale, as in sweet self-conviction which will add a smile to my world, but I cannot undo you - we both have learned to encase ourselves in modest love, and learned to appreciate it to its end, as if it were a miracle. And is that not true divinity?

*And what would divinity feel without the audience of its lovers?*

*Would it even exist without its lovers' hearts?*

*And if we can descend from those heights to the truth, we must ask: is an unloved person even alive?*

You would have to take a pill of forgetfulness for these thoughts, or alternatively ask the scientists for a love pill and distribute it to the masses, to gather under his wings even the many lost and strugglers who yearn so much, those who seek not divinity, but are content with small flashes.

*How rare love is!*

See the wonderful nature, and in it that beautiful flower, the Queen of the Night, which is hidden from existence most days, and expresses itself for only one night, in which it both blooms and withers. From beginning to end it becomes a masterpiece in its beauty and the addictive, dominant scent it exudes. Imagine its crass thoughts.

*For so long I've waited for that moment, and it quickly approaches.*

**But who will be your audience?**

*I don't need an audience. The thing in itself is the point.*

**And what is the thing?**

*Being beautiful.*

**But who will appreciate your beauty? Who will enjoy it?**

*Why should you aim for a purpose or a compliment? I am beautiful and that is enough.*

**What if all would miss your special night?**

*What if I had never been? Give yourself to my essence and do not pride yourself in heights. Be beautiful and love yourself in contentment.*

It is enough to fall in love with the modest colors of a flower, which is a masterpiece regardless of the gaze of its surrounding. It is magical love, even before it blooms is aware that in the future, and so soon, it will wither.

*A person has a mission in life, and that is to know the lights of his spirit, even if he were forever hidden from others in Plato's cave.*

# What do I see in me?

# Chapter Six:
## THE PLAY OF LIFE

◆ ◆ ◆

I would like to watch their life's play...

**Whose?**

Does it matter? Each and every one. Just watch them in an imaginary theater, which is never to be. In such a theater we could sit and watch man's every action from the moment of his birth. Surprisingly, we could also delve into the recesses of his mind, view all of his experiences in the play which is his life, and even have total access to his infinite thoughts and emotions at every given moment. A complete documentation of the inner turmoils of his mind. We can even go as far as his hidden subconscious, which causes a person to mislead his mind in unexplained oblivion.

**Why is such an exposure so curious to you? Did you want to watch the play of your own life? Will you be brave enough to give others tickets to such a screening?**

Why do you project that on me?

**It is you who speaks to me, is it not? In any case, try and confront my question from within you.**

It is terrible. For all of my crudest thoughts would suddenly be naked and I could not hide in the least. What would be of privacy? I would surely faint and fall, inwardly ashamed of my wretched thoughts, and I can no longer eliminate them for they are from within me! All is exposed!

**Such an existential exposure must be terrible for you, but you should not forget how intriguing it would be to watch you and your mind in the most total sense possible.**

Surely I would cry in front of everyone. Could I not? For they will know how terrible my thoughts are at difficult times, and how could I look them in the eyes again? How could I carry on living? And even were I charming in certain thoughts, would they judge me favorably? I know my world well, and without recounting all my deeds I know fully well that there is more terror than wonder in me.

**Men quickly judge horrible events. But don't forget that they will also be aware of your original thoughts. And they would appreciate your sorrow and your reprieve, which, even if not heard outwardly, must have evolved into internal regret.**

I have already thought that these viewers will act humanely and with intimate naivety. For well they know that others can also watch their own life and the depths of their winding psyche. And if so - they might be biased and see in my life their own world, too. It is well known that everything in the other reflects, in different shades, your own world.

**Moreover - man has extreme thoughts about anything his eyes see, and how can we judge him? By his heart's intentions, or by the result of his actions?**

*We must stop acting as a court for human souls. The brave have agreed to let us pry into their souls, and by that have given us their world, and for that - for the rarity of this act - we will forgive them everything.*

It is one thing that a person wishes to watch the life-play of strangers, but how exciting would it be for a grieving person to be allowed an exception, to watch the life-play of his loved ones? Just like knowing in the deepest sense how he was so loved, how he was truly seen and how central was his role in this unique, one-time, life-play of his loved ones.

*Beware that thought! I cannot think of a price that would be too dear for me to pay to be able to watch my loved ones' life-play!*

See how this question drives loving yearnings and eternal longings in us. For suddenly this existential question kicks us into the lives of others, as if we were with our parents from the first moments of our creation and could see their eyes full of love for us, their first caress on our cheeks, the gentle kisses of our nose and the endless battles they had fought for us. There you have true love, eternally documented.

*Such heights we have not yet known, for a person is exposed in the play of his own life only to the so filtered contents of others. And here, suddenly, the entire rainbow of their emotions would be clear to him, from the most terrible to the most wonderful. But will he be brave enough to also recognize his loved ones' darkest thoughts towards him? Can he contain them in him? Or perhaps this existential threat makes clear to us the facility by which others accept various faiths of forgiveness and cleansing from on high? For they are well aware of their actions from without and their thoughts from within, and are so concerned of being judged by others.*

Why go so far? Take part in an intimate, embracing, perspective. Fictions are not for us. Should we add another brilliant invention, a magical remote, with which we can skip to desired scenes, as knowing that these would be the purest and would add so much charm to our world... We have already said in a previous discussion that not every truth should be known.

*Will you let me watch your life's play?*

With great love. You already know the secrets of my soul, and these would surely be more wonderful than all of my most terrible thoughts put together. And you know me, for our being is one and thoughts embrace you as if you could not enjoy the projects of existential suffering in a man's soul. You know how to distance the guilty thoughts of others, and you have considered your life's play a masterpiece, scored and scratched as it may be. As a person, you know yourself intimately.

*Inwardly, I smile deeply when hearing these words. In them you have proven your love and acceptance of me. For it is I speaking from within you... Is it possible to give self-love? And you have considered your life's play a masterpiece... could it be?!*

It seems that the conclusions our mind draws from this conversation seek to return to mother's wisdom in saying that "there are no awards at the end of life's play". And remember that this life is a gift, and that it is universally accepted, as any child would confirm, that a gift is yours to play with as you see fit.

# How would you feel in a staging of your life's play?
# Is there someone you would let watch it?

# Chapter Seven:
## FATHER

––––––––––––––––––––––––––

◆ ◆ ◆

He seeks to eradicate his own existence!

**Eradicate his own existence how? And why?**

He said that his existence demeans his spirit, that because of his disability he cannot even think up possible forms of suicide - and this in itself boils the blood in his heart to the point of despair.

**What did you say to such harsh words?**

Tears fill the void. I cannot contend with a loved one who seeks to eradicate his own existence, but at the same time I know that I could not understand his reality. For I knew his spirit in other days, when he was a complete person, active in spirit and in the presence of others. And now, not only is he closed off inside four walls, but old friends are drawing away, as if afraid that someday they will be like him. This, too, he could express to my eyes.

I will say something more. There were moments when he said: I would not have my life but for you. For otherwise I would be alone in the world. And how should I contend with such words? How much loneliness is in them?

**Such penetrating words express the existential connection between you, whether you wanted them to or not. For we could not ignore it for any price. And his tears, that are now aimed to receive your comfort, they were your young tears at other times, when he embraced you.**

And even though I take it upon myself to be there for him in any matter he asks of me, in me I still know that there are moments when he is alone, and terrible thoughts squirm within him on the matter of becoming a half-person. It is as if he lost his hold and is dependant on my graces. And it is possible that his thoughts wonder whether I will disappear and he will at last be alone in the world - how terrifying is that thought!

**Relieve yourself of such thoughts. Remember that your mind holds similar ones, and see how happy you are together when you can charm each other with ideas, or to be silent together. For you had the privilege to learn the highest knowledge of existence, which is to appreciate things before they are lost, when his existence was almost eradicated in the past.**

I bring these thoughts before him, and frankly I can see in his eyes how happy he can be for a few moments, which he grasps to their end, and how terrible it is to leave him and go back to my own life, to my own loneliness and my own adventures, those I share with him, and he enjoys listening to every detail. They remind him of his old world.

How wonderful it is for him to take part in your decisions! By that he lives a little, has influence as he was used to, he is still your father!

How strange our love is! As you can imagine, even his ability to converse is not as it was. At times he struggles to find the right word, and instead fires a completely arbitrary one, and we both burst into contagious laughter, as if crying out, with a smile, the wretched terror of life. We feel very close then.

Smile and humor were always a healing love-drug.

And at times wonderful magics happen and another unexpected happiness surprises his soul. Imagine what kind of excitement happen in him, when he pronounces a new word, which had not been said for many years. As if he brought it into the world for the first time. Thousands of words have abandoned him and disappeared from him in the stroke he experienced. He did not even know if they would ever come back. And what is strangest? That the funniest, clearest words he has are profanities. Yes, of all the words in the world it is profanities that he most successfully retained.

It is a high and important artistic capability.

How strange it is to love a person who no longer holds on to being a person? And how terrifying…

Moreover, I also know that his love for me would be very limited, as if even the expectation to receive the greatest love a father can give to his son, which is his faith in him, were unraveled.

How far will you go?

I still know and feel inside me that this need has suddenly abandoned me, as if I were a creation which is not dependant on the faith of others. But I also know that him becoming a half-person made it easier for me to deal with my own needs.

**How so?**

You have here a reality where life is turned on its head: the child became the parent and the parent became the child. This turnaround changes the direction of the play, and now natural needs disappear by the force of reality, and the winding soul bewitches itself when faced with each terrible struggle, as if it sought to find light in the darkness which so crassly overtakes it. And I wonder further: If a man is not given guidance on how to be a man, how can a father, without guidance, know how to be a father?

**It seems that you came across an existential absurdity. And you could let other people serve as meaningful parents, even though some of them you have never met, but only read about.**

Definitely! Some of them are so magical that they have become a loving and meaningful tribe for me, for I have faced the absurd and accepted the burden of randomness which has touched me, and I was forced to find a way to deal with the terror of life - and I feel proud of that. I am not willing to be lost, even though I was disappointed of my deepest needs.

**It seems people have powers of spirit, which includes unending reservoirs of strength that can withstand every terror.**

Love can withstand every terror.

**Or is it terror that intensifies the heart's emotions?**

This combination is particularly enchanted at times of distress, and how

commonplace are the human tragedies that prove this throughout history.

**And it is exactly the terrified, the one whose existential choices were so diminished, that is the one to ascend to the heroism of meaning. His spirit is able to sort his world as a surgeon does, and by that recreate the order of things and find the subjoot for which life is still worthy of living, even if external.**

And even if we are so afraid to be like him, we will yet admire how mentally

active he is at all times, even now.

**And what of you? Can you imagine what father-figure you will be to your future children?**

Hard questions!

I will teach them loving life-hacks.

# Did you have any other significant parents?

# Chapter Eight:
## AN INTERNAL MIRROR

◆ ◆ ◆

**Where does your soul turn to, my friend?**

*Definitely to my wonderful loved ones, to those in whose play of life I took part, as an actor. I have so many feelings towards them, as if without them I would be a completely different person. And at the same time I wonder whether they feel the same towards me. For a person only truly discusses himself as a singular phenomenon, and inwardly I asked that others will perceive my world as an indistinguishable part of theirs.*

**Is it not natural to recognize a person's desire to be intimately known by their loved ones, as if they had become a meaningful person for them? What is recognition if not a gentle compliment that embraces a person's consciousness and saves them from a vacuous feeling that clings to one who is no longer needed by others?**

*Deeper emotions still rise in me: who of all my loved ones truly sees me?*

**What do you mean?**

We already know that each and every one of us is a unique and wonderful instance of life, one that has never been. But my mind immediately wisened up to me and asks: unique to who? To me, judging myself? I want to be unique to them, to my loved ones! Is that not a modest demand for any man?

**Of course it is. But see how many souls there are whose full depths no man truly sees. They pass through the world and from it without any feeling or attachment, as if they were a silent breeze, as if they never even were. And from within our soul we must surely know how deep is a person's desire to express his world and by that save himself from those damn masks which he so well hides behind at all times.**

Despite our words, it is clear to everyone that even if a man's desire to be recognized acts within him in winding paths, still he must not necessarily be capable of a complete exposure, as if aware that it would not flatter him. But in his modest way he seeks recognition at least for the good in his world. And he is not like those whose pride knows no bounds and seek recognition even from those completely strange to them, and put their names on plaques and banners. Some also seek acceptance after their death, as if they could derive some pleasure from others' thoughts of them when they are gone. Can you imagine such a thing? So strange are humans...

**So very strange. But it is a sign that we all contend with something. I was thinking, perhaps a person's greatest contention is to receive acceptance from within, and not be dependant on the judgement of others. But this demand cannot be put to anyone but the most brave.**

Perhaps at times it is great heroism not to be brave at all. Particularly in this war, I admit that I do not have the fortitude for that. A man seeks to be loved as a child who is always cared for and adored. And how strange are humans, that the more they grow up they demand more and more love, but can only find less and less.

**This is why that feeling is so rare, when she turned to your eyes and said: I truly see you. As the greatest embrace that can be asked for.**

How rare is such exposure for a person? Inwardly he was afraid that as soon as he would be naked, figuratively, in front of others - they will run away as if from a plague. But it is also possible that a close eye contact will allow them to truly see you, from the terrible to the wonderful in you, a gaze that will not be afraid to embrace your life's play.

**What is that if not love?**

And another thought I have, that a person walks the journey of life and hides most of his steps as if he held to his first steps and his last movements, but that most of his spirit's journey he has hidden from himself under the barrage of social demands. But in this miraculous event, in which his inner world is present, he can suddenly walk proudly and accepts the support of the audience, which is also aware of the rarity of this feeling of love, and especially its absence in their world.

**And what of those who no one really sees?**

They express a gentle longing for a mirror, even a small one. Just so they see something.

**Even a spark?**

Even a gaze.

# Who truly sees you in this play of life?

# Chapter Nine:
## HIDDEN NEEDS

◆ ◆ ◆

I asked people about my wants, and they demanded that I know my internal needs myself. Yet, I could not express them. For until now I was only aware of their needs, and was filled with happiness seeing their smiles.

**And how is it possible for a man to look inwards to the gentleness in his soul, while building walls and towers against his own intelligence? Intelligence that seeks a hidden path in, but is immediately felled by his cutting conscience, which is accustomed to give in to others, just so as not to embrace his own spirit, as a lover embraces a loved one.**

Suddenly I asked myself which roles I fill in their world, and which roles I would ask them to fill for me. This question has secretly penetrated through the many obstacles I have set myself, and suddenly I realized that my world was enslaved to understand the many spirits of my loved ones, while I have lost myself.

**And how modest are the demands of your own spirit?**

I asked them to give a smile and look favorably on my life's play, as if they took part in both the terrible and the wonderful in me. And I also gently asked that *they express in words my meaning in their world, and know that I could appreciate the small deeds just as much as the very great ones, as in the days when I wondered how I came to embrace so fully, and I found that I have missed those deeds in the past. And what kind of great trick has happened when I expressed this need to my loved ones? Suddenly they afforded me embraces, filled with thousands of gentle words, their fingers caressing the soul which yearned for it so.*

It seems that it takes great courage for a man to express the needs of his soul, first to himself and then to others. But past experience dictates that others do not only come closer by his exposure, but that they also perceive him as a present soul, not to be used only for their own needs and wants. Suddenly he becomes a subject, as a clear and powerful essence: I am here.

*And I will further add that my demands are aimed at emotions, and I already knew that the heart cannot ignore an honest and exposed intent, as a magic rule that resolves to good, honest eyes.*

A person will seek his loved one to be so intimate with him that she could distinguish the subtle tones of his mind, that she will fight his war to the appropriate degree, and that he will fight hers - and together they both hold each other as they stride forward in the play of life. But this is not always reality, and at times one person's soul finds refuge in another's, and is lost in it, as if it found wonderful solace from the hardships of life, and forgot that its loved one is also in an existential war, and loves her soul more than his own. In this process he assumes that his love is worthy, and that even the price of his self-sacrifice is!

And perhaps we shall go even further, because at times it is proper that a man lay down his soul for some time, since he is required to tend to those of his loved ones. But how long can he forget himself? How resilient would he be?

And moreover, I know that he cannot continue to hide in this way forever, for he himself is fighting the flames of existence, and even though he hides under his devotion to her, he is still full of yearning for a similar feeling of acceptance and intimacy, and cannot be otherwise.

*And how wonderful it is for him when his soul receives the place it truly deserves and his complete world is exposed and expressed to the extremes of its terror and wonder? How would he feel when a complete soul seeks to see him, just as he has been used to seeing others?*

And yet some find in us specks of light that we were not aware of, or couldn't recognize.

*How does that happen?*

A person is used to wander the forest of his loved ones' souls as a brave companion, with whom they agree to lose themselves. But how strange and peculiar would it be for him to find a soul he would be able to be lost in, a soul who would wander in his forest and hold his gentle hand as if whispering: "trust me, I will be good to you…" And he replies with a firm grip, never to be loosened lest it will never return, and they walk among the high trees. And only her eyes see the way, see him inwardly in the shades of his own forest, tones hidden from himself.

*So beautiful to suddenly be lost…*

And perhaps my acquaintances will also tell you that it is dangerous for a person to go astray in the souls of others, for those can overcome his own. But I will fiercely object and say that it is better for a person to burn himself ten times, if by that he can authentically express the fibers of his heart even once, as in a magical assimilation, soul to soul, in an embrace closer than both the terrible and wonderful in him.

Definitely.

**Will I be so bold as to ask you now for your own needs?**

But by that you have expressed the question that every lover must ask his own loved ones, as if he sought to come close to them, to truly see them inwardly... And how rare is this question among humans? As if they assumed beforehand that everything is clear and simple and there is no need to delve into the obvious. But in our intimate discussion we have slowly eliminated the terror which hides in the obvious.

**You rush to comprehend my words. So I will repeat my question and ask to know your true needs to their finest nature. Is that possible?**

Certainly, for I have nothing but you, for you are myself.

And if we agreed on that, I have now asked to distinguish my most hidden needs and my natural limitations. And the highest of them is perhaps my so deep desire to know that their love to me depends on nothing, as if it were above and below, beyond every faith and limitation, as if I were standing beyond high ideas and values. Or in other words - as I love them.

**Like a knife to the heart.**

For true lovers stand fast, armed against any attempt to risk any of their loved ones, is that not so?

Of course it is. A sensitive yearning for a person to have at least one place in the world in which stability will be infinite, as a refuge from the clamorous burdens of existence. Where he could have the good embracing eyes of pure goodness. One must appreciate this sensation to its fullest.

*From my short experience with life, I have learned that I am unable to sustain all of my loved ones' needs. And the more I exposed my needs from them - we were left in certain helplessness, for there is deep disappointment in that. And on the other hand - a feeling of relief words cannot describe. Suddenly we felt to the bone the pure love that exists between us, and have shed the fiction that everyone knows, but hide in a sin of shame, that their loved ones' would forever be complete perfection for them.*

It seemed that we overestimated our virtues, and couldn't be modest with those qualities that do exist in us.

*And when I truly acknowledged this truth, I could release myself from childish expectations and focus on loving traits, such as accepting the person in front of me as they truly are, from a mature understanding that we all try to handle the tempest of life even before our shared journey.*

## What are our hidden needs?

# Chapter Ten:
## LEARNING TO LIVE

♦ ♦ ♦

It seems that a person's path winds between their dreams and their fragile reality. While they still walk the earth, their thoughts are not concerned with their present world, but rather with its end, which draws near at breakneck speed, as if they tried to deny it, yet were aware of their failure in that task.

**And were I to sneak into the consciousness of that man, I would surely look into it and ask which is the greater fear: The fear to die, or perhaps the fear to finally live?**

And moreover, that person seeks to outsmart themselves. For they have expressed an intimate thought: the fear of dying is not as great as they thought, and is enchanted in his mind because they do not know how to live.

**Be careful with those words, for who will teach a person how to live, or more precisely - how to die?**

These two extremes are very near each other, and it seems that in a very crude and surprising way, this is where a person can hold both ends of the stick. For knowing how to die, they would surely know how to live, and knowing how to live, their death would certainly be received with complete understanding.

And were they not well versed in these crafts, they would surely spend their life in a feeling of non-being, as if they existed only *in absence*.

How can you exist in absence?

Do you not listen to the words of old men? So many describe how they blatantly missed so many years of their lives, which can clearly no longer be returned. And you could not doubt their mere existence for all those lost years. They truly were, but only *in absence*.

Shall we show compassion to our souls, and accept a loss of one year for every ten we have lived? Or is this too lenient? Perhaps a person loses half of their life?

Stop expressing more of the terror in me! Let us return to the sacred learning, the one that will clarify to us how I could die in the best and most beautiful manner, and by that also live as I sought to be.

It seems that you would have asked the philosopher to gather the crowd in the marketplace and to expressly indicate the proper death. And at first did not even understand why they should hear such trivialities, for how can they discuss what does not exist in their minds?!

Let them be. Talk to me, to yourself. Be with me for one moment, as close as possible. Tell me a great secret from within you.

It seemed to be an impossibly winding whirlpool that I have known from within me, for I am willing to die each day anew, as if to know and appreciate my world to its fullest before its absence.

*And how can you die each day anew?*

**Ask yourself the inverse: what predated what - light or dark? Which of the two supports its contradiction? Who better describes life: the dead, or those living in their absence?**

*It is clear that those who have seen the end expose the mask of life in a clearer,*

*sharper way than those who live in their absence. But so enchanted is their path,*

*now that they can no longer speak.*

**But see what cunning of the mind your mouth expressed: even in our discussions I do not truly exist. It is only you, expressing yourself in a different form in your imagination. And perhaps here, too, you can animate the mouths of those who are no longer among the living, as if they would tell you hidden, wonderful things?**

*What would those tell me?*

**They would require you for a task only a few are capable of.**

*Enough of your concealment!*

**Viktor Frankl would express to you the most charming thought ever written. In his book, Man's Search for Meaning, he demands of the reader to "live as if you were living already for the second time and as if you had acted for the first time as wrongly as you are about to act now."[1]**

*So crass are those who are already gone, but still seek to educate? Where were*

*they and their wisdom when they were alive? Is this demand not a blatant proof*

*of their absence in their lives?*

---

[1] Viktor E. Frankl, *Man's Search for Meaning,* (Boston: Beacon press, 1964), p. 50, trans. Ilse Lasch.

True. Only the dead can educate with such enchanted advice. And perhaps it is the imagination of a man who converses with his older image, as you do...

Perhaps we shall continue to converse with the dead, and they will enchant us with more biting thoughts?

How beautiful will be the conversation of the great geniuses who are already digesting their wisdom not in their active soul but after the fact! Imagine a series of their lectures after their life's play, completely free of the familiar borders.

I would have asked for one cutting line from each, and by that I would certainly learn to die in the best way.

And in that it still seems that when a man is painfully conscious of his nearing end, then his world cleanses to the point that he would fall in love with his dreams, and his termination would be a surprise upon coming.

Would those agree on a few modest commandments, for which a person could die, and therefore also live not in his absence? And how beautiful are their deliberations on such matters, as if they extracted spirit by sharing cutting wisdom? They would turn the world of psychology on its head in one hour's worth of talking!

These geniuses would create the most enchanted book of books, as if making obsolete all other wonderous creations by combining their ideas. Can you imagine the wonderous hall where Nietzsche, Dostoyevsky, Freud, Sartre, Tolstoy, Yeshayahu Leibowitz and others would gather?

Oh dear, I almost fell in love with my existence in this moment. For it will take a whole life for me to experience my world and give in to the depths of their sacred souls. And it seems now that concerning myself with high ideals can make my life worthwhile, and so I will not live only in absence and by submitting to the common fictions, but I will become a masterpiece in myself, with the advice of the most wonderful masterpieces humanity has ever known.

# What is the most enchanting thought you have heard?

# Chapter Eleven:
## AN INNER DREAM

◆ ◆ ◆

Something so strange has happened in me.

**What could it have been?**

I dreamed of you.

**And how could you have imagined my face?**

I saw my young face talking to your aging image and could not contain my
emotions. It is so rare in the universe that crying eyes meet.

**A shiver runs down my spine when I imagine your hands wrapped around
my face as if we knew each other.**

Would you have known me had you seen me in the street?

**Would *you* have known *me*?**

How exciting would it have been, a meeting between the young man and his
older image? And I immediately asked myself about my loved ones who would
meet their younger image... they would have surely embraced no end!

They would have cried and expressed wonderful love to themselves. And see how enchanted is that thought of yours, for there is love in it.

How can that be?

How wonderful it is for a person to imagine his aging self, and how they share intimate phrases, as if to clarify his most hidden desires, or alternatively to try and imagine which words were addressed specifically to him.

What is so special about that?

The very fact of your dream expresses intimate longing. How rare it is for a person to observe his later spirit, as an extremely talented painter who foresees his future portrait! For a person looks at the mirror and sees himself, and imagines what terror must rise up when a young man suddenly sees his aging face in the mirror?

Oh dear... does your eye, at least, still charm hearts?

When we agree to intimately know our anxiety, there is much charm in it.

How terrible and disabling are such thoughts to a person contending with difficulties, for he can suddenly look and feel the gentle wrinkles in that being of his, so strange and distant. But suddenly in the dream he can really touch. And when he truly touches, the heart reverses and shrinks - and there's wonderful liberation in it.

And let's delve deeper into these wrinkles in me, the ones that bring nausea and worries to you, the young man. It was immediately when you caressed my coarse skin, as little sand dunes which will soon disappear in the wind - that you saw the existential dread. For you have truly touched me, and therefore also felt it to the flesh. You have seen yourself in me, and you immediately knew that you have time no end to choose otherwise, to be you as much as you want.

And perhaps in my dream I watched you and smiled with simple agreement, for your world flatters my dreams, and I was proud of you that your path was my own.

Either way, dreams express in a person their well hidden wisdom, and it is drawn in infinitely gorgeous colors. And I will immediately examine in me whether I ever dreamed of you, your young blue eyes, my experiences you had - and I found that I have endlessly missed the paths and possibilities that lay before me. In truth... I miss you.

You...

Miss...

And now, where else would I turn my thoughts towards? I knew well that for all of the imaginations in my mind, with you... with myself, for all of these I still wished to look into your deep eyes and try and imagine in my spirit what you enjoy these days, what bothers you and what brings a smile to your face.

I want to meet you so!

Do not rush time... You will surely still sit in this chair and remember that so contemporary world of yours.

At once, a no less enchanting thought emerged: what if I meet the boy I was... It is just as writing a letter to our young being... and what wonderful cure it is *for a man to come close to one of his other characters in his wonderful and unique journey through the play of life?*

# How would the encounter with your older self look?

## What would you talk about?

# Chapter Twelve:
## WHO AM I?

♦ ♦ ♦

I often wondered at how many thoughts I have, and how few words. Where does my soul find full expression? When it is turned towards me, or towards others? And moreover, I contemplated how humans spend most of their days inside themselves, even though they wish to be together. Now it is no longer clear to me who I truly am.

Imagine a person who remains silent throughout his life, only conversing with himself. Is there a better partner than his own being?

Of course, for if I could not express my world to you, what would I have been to myself? If it weren't for the environment that challenges my world, what would I have been?

You would have been helpless, and that is a horrible feeling.

And what is there for the lonely person? He does not truly have someone to talk to except for himself, and characters with different voices appear in him, who speak amongst themselves on various matters. But who truly decides in his practical life? Who sets the tone? Who is the true Self between the numerous characters in his mind?

Is this not the theater of life in which a person plays various characters in his mind, and outwardly represents just one major role? How dire is the loneliness of the person who for most of his existence was nothing but the audience watching his own life's play?

Where is the wisdom in such enchanted questions? Help me find solace, be a worthy director of my own life's play.

Be yourself amidst your own characters and accept the burden of existential loneliness. Only by that you could appreciate the company of your friends, the ones who themselves are so eager for an audience in their life's theater. They too live in silence amidst their various characters, seeking solace among the crowd.

How could you know that? Do all men truly hold a cast of characters in their mind, who aids them to contend with loneliness? Is that the reality of the struggling person?

Turn your gaze inwards and you will see: people are so alike that you would think they will learn compassion.

If I would learn to understand my existential loneliness, which forces me to accept that even though I will be loved no end, still only my conversations with myself will be wholly understood. Only the person himself can see his mind completely. His friends can only go so far, and no farther.

And even if you faced those of the outmost genius and infinite sensitivity even if you had the ability to express yourself to the highest degree - still you would always be alone in your finest thoughts, the ones that no man but you can ever understand.

How did you become so vain as to determine that I must contend with myself without the aid of a friend? They understand me to the core, for I strip bare before them!

Even if we could analyze the soul, as if it were an exact science, even then certain wirings only you know of would be hidden from observers. For you cannot divulge this information to anyone, and it is possible that this information is hidden even from you.

Then how different are the experiences of a person who can express words to the millions, and of one who has never uttered a single word from within his soul? After all, both of them are lonely in their being. Both of them are completely alone... Moreover, it seems that those who are silent are the ones who have accepted the burden of loneliness, while those whose speech never ends merely deny their loneliness in long mutterings.

Do not be a hero for silence. It is good for a person to share their spirit with loved ones, and even embarass themselves in front of strangers. There is a good fight in that. But beforehand, you must recognize in yourself that only you can truly see your light. Or think of it this way: what is falling in love other than seeing yourself in another's soul? Suddenly and wordlessly you have seen the loneliness of your thought in her world, as if you silently shared a conversation.

As if I repressed a thought that only I knew and never told anyone, and saw that she has the same one. A person falls in love with himself in his love for her, as if he took root in her.

**Don't rush to such malicious thoughts. Think simply to me, I am close by.**

*Do you understand? Did you feel that? At times my thoughts are so quick that they jump undistinguishably from the most terrible to the most wonderful. And it is so marvelous that your character is here with me for a moment, to stop and watch.*

**One must dwell. One must pause for a moment and be.**

*Where is the pause in the cast of characters in a man's soul? There is no pause. It is a show that never stops, characters are ceaselessly replaced in a range of animated discussion. You seek a pause and I ask: by what right? The audience seeks entertainment!*

**At times you must kick up a racket, stop everything and observe. Be in firm consciousness to the core. To be silent as death, or to uncontrollably scream in the forest. You must be the leading actor and you can perform a beautiful, silent, soliloquy such as have never been. Will you be brave enough to keep silent?**

*I am barely brave enough to speak.*

## Which better expresses you?
## Your thoughts? Your words?

# Chapter Thirteen:
## AN IMPORTANT MEETING.

◆ ◆ ◆

I've seen them all!

*Who?*

Don't you understand? I have seen them all!

*What are we talking about?*

At night I dreamed of all the significant people who have accompanied me from childhood to damned old age.

*How could that be? Where can one order such a marvelous dream?*

I could not describe it but from within. I was sitting in the middle of a large circle and was enveloped by hundreds of wonderful people who approached me with kind words, as if sharing their world with me. My soul shuddered and my heart began to shrink inside, for it is known that only so a person perishes in his sleep... This frightened me to wakefulness, and I returned from the nothingness.

*Who was there? Do I know them all?*

You know only a few, for you still have long to live, and they will surprise your world only later. But do not seek windows to the future, for you will not believe the words of those you already know.

*What did they say?*

I could not expose their world to you, for your own dream would still surprise you in old age.

*Well... you can at least tell me who you have seen there.*

I have **seen** there your close family, your great loves, the pianists who enchant your soul and even Vivaldi, your greatest love. With a hidden smile I will also say that even Jessy, the ginger dog whose wonderful stories move you to the extreme, was there.

*How so? I thought only people I knew in my own life were there, and suddenly*

*you tell me that there were also such distinguished guests, who have infinitely*

*influenced me even though I have never met them? I envy your dream so much;*

*how will I meet those in order to give them my endless appreciation?*

How exciting was it to meet those we have loved so much that we lost ourselves? Hearing their words, I filled myself with tears. They have loved you and lost themselves in you, and there are still evidence you cannot hide left on the flesh of your soul. And their colorful eyes are still as beautiful exactly as they were when you fell in love with their gentle souls.

*Is that not a terrible trick? By the force of these eyes I so quickly fall in love, and*

*still they are left full of masterful paintings... like being lost in a forested island.*

Can you imagine how they embraced me?

Can you imagine a love greater than two pair of eyes finding each other before the show ends?

I am still trying to process my feelings when meeting all of them in that hall. But inwardly I know that I will be so excited that I'll faint. How can a man contain so many loves at one and the same time? And still more terrible, they are different loves, in so deep and enchanted layers that human words cannot even describe.

And I will also tell you that in my dreams I could not speak one word until they have all come in, one by one. Can you imagine that? They have all come in the same order in which they have entered my life, and at the same time my eyes met my loved ones, an infinity of moments I have been with them immediately surfaced in me... and I smiled a teary smile.

Surely more meaningful figures have entered the space, such who have had an infinitely large influence on my life without me even being aware of their work. For each person has his own saviors throughout his life's play, of whose nobility he is unaware, and whose actions are ever-present.

Do you remember the smiling old man whose hospital bed was next to your father's? Do you remember watching them playing chess wordlessly?

Do you remember the number tattooed on his arm?

Do you remember his wisdom to you? That he said: "In life, one cannot stand still, one must keep moving." His words were forever etched in your heart.

What are these wonderous secrets?! So many phrases are etched into a person's soul, without them knowing their origin. There must be some magical root to all of that. Have I thanked those who have cultivated worlds in me?

Let that be. For all of them would not have come to a special gathering in my dream were they full of anger towards you, would they? If so - they must have come together by their love to you and your love to them, out of honest smiling eyes and moments of happinnes, small and large, in hidden words as in a great adventure, in a long lovers' trip and in the smiles of children who appreciate their world to no end.

Have you met my children there?

What questions!

They must have been as colorful as I am!

It is strange indeed how most of your loved ones were of colorful spirit, and in most cases, also appearance.

But is that not merely a coincidence?

And what solace do coincidences give? It is man who makes things coincide.

Well then, I like colorful people!

At the end I stood up and walked around the hall, looking deeply into their eyes lest I miss one of them, and felt completely in existence. And in one second they were gone and disappeared in my consciousness, and I woke up, a lake of tears on my cheeks.

I had another thought, that your dream expresses man's anxiety of the oblivion which bites indistinguishably into the stores of his memory. And what is a man if not the sum of his memories? And the older he becomes the more hours of reality are lost from his winding consciousness, as in a play in which the audience misses long moments of every scene. And how could he guess? How could he express helplessness regarding the memories in the lake of nothingness? The more information he misses, the more he gives in to falsification, to a deforming and redrawing of his needs, or alternatively, meets his real world through the same gathering in your dreams, among the numbers of those who take the most prominent part in your being.

Will you cast more doubt on the reliability of the speakers in my dream? One can also imagine that I put words into their mouth, and they were merely extras, used to stir emotions. Would you seek to show that a person, in their inner conversations, was also the director of other characters aside from fulfilling the lead role?

I am not brave enough to go there, but things are clear and I have determined that people contend with a variety of remarkable distresses, and for those they learn how to better express the creative solutions in their souls. That is - a person, by his nature, heals.

Let go of that. Take part in my dream, be one of my guests and tell me loving, smiling words. Take part in my anxieties, take hold of my hand and never let go.

# Who will take part in your most important encounter?

# Chapter Fourteen:
## THE FACTORIES OF THE SOUL

I cannot understand how is it that I have an endless reservoir of memories on which I can draw at any time, but seemingly with almost no control on that matter. Worlds within me which I sought to forget may crop up and rise up to my gentle consciousness. I immediately asked: where am *I* in this whole story?

**It is only you, is it not?**

I'm not entirely convinced now. If for one moment we contemplate that I am the sole ruler of my soul, I would immediately ask what benefit do I gain from the painful longing to a once-beloved? I am trying to contend and overcome them! What benefit all these memories have to healing my soul? Perhaps it is this theater of life whose program is a cursed drama, as if it must generate upheavals against all odds?

At times it truly seems that the human spirit contains factories, each producing a separate and independent emotion. Each and every one of these is able, in one gentle moment, to change a person's world. In these factories we employ workers according to the outline of our lives. Many employ thousands of workers in the factory of guilt, others have but few workers for love, and instead delve only into themselves, and we all move along different axes, each person and his own spirit. And there are also tall heroes, able to fire thousands of workers with one magical decision, and even recruit some for special assignments.

And if my heart has endless love for her? Many workers in the realm of my memories are tied to her and cannot be severed. They are not only mine. They have been linked to her spirit as well, in an inexplicable cooperation. These do not leave me, for souls are forever linked, as if it were still possible to imagine that were we to meet each other many years from now, we would still be excited by the journey of memories, which is nothing but an amazing and exciting spectacle of two loving people.

It seems to be part of the rules of the game, my friend. A person who can reach loving heights can also fall to the most painful and hurtful lows. It is no wonder, then, that these longing memories assault your mind, for they express in you the highs you so crave. And what can be more wonderful to a man than his loved ones' smile as they embrace his world? How can one even compare this moment to their daily routine which goes by as a blurred movie they watch from the cheap seats, while they so yearn for the lead role!

And were I to let myself delve even deeper, I might raise another contemplation, that perhaps there is even some joy in my mind from these thoughts?

How could you enjoy it?

Since a person, in his winding thought, can live such events again as if they were existing reality, as if repressing the obvious truth. And if they cannot deal with existing reality, they can live in the illusions of their thoughts, as if those are their own reality.

**These are terrible thoughts, how far will you go?**

Well, I don't consider them in daily life, but I know the human mind. When one loves so much that they blend into another, they might even reach that point.

**Why would you hide under another? Expose your world to me.**

I asked thousands of loving workers to erect a green and colorful garden for all those magical years in which I learned to fill the emotional factory in my spirit.

**I could look into your eyes and see that it is not your private factory alone, for a person is always in some space, and workers from different factories co-operate in creating the wonderful, as well as the terrible - and how proud must loving workers of both sides be that they are able to embrace each other despite their employers' inevitable wars.**

And in another tone - what is the appearance of the factory in the mind of a depressed man? Are loving workers fired wholesale? Or perhaps those of blame and self-loathing recruited?

**These are extreme poles, but what of the common man? The one who wakes up every day to his own reality, and suddenly life puts extreme demands, one way or another, on his factory? How could he assign workers to the right places?**

Ah, questions!

We still know how to express other extreme hardships, in which the factory is like a tempest raging in a great container, and life is so lost that it would seek to shut down as in fainting tremors.

Did you remember the heart's embrace you gave in such harsh moments?

A non-relenting embrace!

This is evidence that each factory manager must have loved-ones nearby, for in difficult times they could serve as support beams for his emotional factory.

## What does your factory look like?

# Chapter Fifteen:
## ON SILENCE

◆ ◆ ◆

**Why are you so silent, young man?**

Better that I be silent than spread too many words, which are not even mine.

**Let that be. So few people truly speak their own words.**

I take no solace in that. When I pay attention to the thoughts that escape through my words, I feel a strong disdain from within me. They do not express my delicate spirit, and the longer my silence lasts, the more my words cannot reach. As if I intended to wonder that perhaps there's nothing in me except for the words of others.

**A terrible and wonderful thought at the same time...**

Even this thought, on the lack of my spiritual content, is not mine. I learned it from the wisdom of others. And how miserable is the person who knows their inner absence?

**It is precisely your recognition of this reality, that a person is always the product of their environment that makes your awareness particularly steadfast. Your silence is full of your own being, even though you are speechless.**

But how longer can one be silent? A person aspires to be something new in the world, but as they grow older they note that they have very few possibilities to enchant in new colors, for all imaginations have already been wonderfully drawn. What novelties can they conjure?

It might only seem so among common people, but in retrospective, the world changes no end in any dimension you look. Still, it seems that these rights are reserved only to a small number! And what of the common people, who are not of high talent? Will they always exist only in the shadow of the living? Will they live in the sense of novelty even though they are far from it?

This is my crudest thought, it is the existential dread in me that I would be a 'nothing' in life itself. I know that I have been a 'nothing' before the day I was born, and even that is no solace. I ask you to be my light.

You do not need lights from within me, for you have expressed the darkness in you so remarkably, and from the depth of your thought you are filled with a great light, even though it is so cleansed that it burns your exposed flesh.

Perhaps now I could accept my silence, for I suddenly gave in to the sounds of the heart as it fills and empties, and I felt the beats of the spirit that winds in me and was, for the first time in my life, a man. As if God watched his creation - and it was suddenly a man watching himself from outside.

But people have the ability to watch themselves inwardly in silence, and hear their gentle, silent voice, which is at times deeper than anything they have said aloud.

But who is even brave enough to be silent? Around me the crowd storms, throwing out its imitated ideas, feeling they are ever new.

And I, as I look and snicker from the sidelines, I project their world onto myself, and understand that despite being so aware, I am also like them, but somewhat different - for they do not feel the anxiety of the 'nothing' that beats in me.

Shall we imagine now a community of meditative silent monks, who give in to their gentle spirit and finally attempt to listen to its silent, intimate words?

But it was a hall full of musicians, shouting their untuned notes, as a vain person whose spirit is completely empty. And in that hall, in a quiet, modest corner, one can hear the gentle sounds of wonderous geniuses... but they are unheard due to the overbearing chaos that prevents a person from seeing their great light, their inner spirit.

Imagine the philosopher shouting and silencing at once the chaos of screams, the hall falls silent for the first time in eons and the gentle sounds are slowly exposed to the ears of the crowd, and their tears burst out inexplicably, as when you are suddenly touched by an insight.

Then, after I have understood my own absence, I would surely be able to value that little part which is truly mine, the treasures hidden in me. And I will give them a place, be aware of what is central and what is incidental in my own life-play.

# How much of your inner world is truly yours?

# Chapter Sixteen:
## SOUL VESSELS

◆ ◆ ◆

**Have you forgotten how to cry?**

I try to smile.

**What do your eyes seek?**

A lake of tears.

**Let it out, then.**

How?

**Unburden. No one is looking.**

My soul has eliminated tears.

**Has it?**

I cried my world out years ago, after the great struggle, and now nothing floods my tear ducts. My soul has grown rigid.

**Do not be harder than need be. There is so much sensitivity in your eyes... Perhaps you cry gently, from your heart and within it.**

By my emotions I know that my experiences in the world are not a boundless space, and therefore they can better express signs in the vessels of my soul.

In early days my tears were raindrops of love, and I could hold them in good proximity, but they have grown so far...

My heart tells me you will yet cry tears of embrace.

Why is that?

I remember well how you were so excited by the gentle words of a maiden who shared with you her inner thoughts of her great love for reading, and the terrible time when her longing for words disappeared, as if her inner spring dried up.

How did I react?

You told her that nothing could hurt your soul more than if all of your beloved books were taken away. At that moment your eyes were reddened and teared uncontrollably.

True, I can still shed tears.

But there is a great desire in you to make yourself cry.

To cry in order to feel my heart beating. It seems that this ability has disappeared from the sum of my qualities, due to the existing defenses and fortifications of my soul, which are nothing but its desire to overcome every enemy.

Surely you have already understood that no real enemy threatens you, and perhaps there is no need to hold on to the same survival strategy that petrified your heart inside a great fortress?

Could it be that the lake of my tears is so beautiful, and that my way to it is blocked by obstacles I have laid myself? Is it possible that people are both their own greatest lover and greatest enemy?

In those times, during the terrible tremor - it was a necessary defensive measure, just as a heartfelt embrace between lovers. But you must not continue to act as if facing terror, for now your world is in a completely different place, a safe and powerful place. You can therefore consider being brave and choosing another strategy, one which will bring you back to that enchanted primacy, that beautiful naivety in your good eyes.

How strange it is for a person to reflect his own soul to himself, without the natural biases of bribery?

And were I brave enough to accept your words, then I would have been forced to face the apex of freedom, which requires me to choose again whether to continue the same behaviour, which was so right for its time but is no longer useful today. And it is obvious to all that there are other paths I can choose today.

A person can change their path and choose to adopt new behaviours if they so desire. Even if it seems that the lake of your tears has been taken over by a spreading desert - rains could still refill it, if you simply allow yourself to shake your hold on that old way of contention.

I can still express my soul, as if it were a dense system of existential vessels that hides all of my world's experiences. And you have recognized that even your stomach cannot hold it all. Imagine a person who meets a horror as it tries to pass through the vessels of his soul? And clearly a person cannot have fortitude enough for all of their wars, and some vessels would be so blocked as to choke and even wound. This can cause a real explosion in a grown person, as tears bursting from the depth of their soul, from an experience that was not properly processed.

At times a person cries without knowing why, a kind of dry tears that seek to rise, not given an appropriate chance earlier.

There is some release in that, is there not? The essence of conversational therapy expresses an attempt to gently look into the vessels of our soul as much as we can, despite the existential concern of an explosion whose results are unknown. As if we could have even imagined that it had been better not to look.

Uncertainty will always accompany a person in this long road, and it is true that there is no evidence that every truth is worthy of being known. But see your tears - today you are brave enough to touch them.

# Can you notice whether your behavior no longer contributes to your happiness and growth?

# Chapter Seventeen:
## A LOVERS' ABSURD

◆ ◆ ◆

How can I comprehend the fact that I have endlessly loved another for such a long time, yet now when our gazes accidently meet in the street the absurd touches us with its terrible sword, as if it had severed ties created by so many years of existential embrace?

And what of the eyes whose loving gaze has turned opaque, as if the emotional cords that have linked your shared world were severed, and the damage was as irreversible as that of a stroke, that forever robs a person of certain abilities?

Colorful eyes have already stopped smiling.

Is that not the most beneficial possibility, as terrible as it is?

How could a person exist while their heart is ever wistful?

They must anesthesize their soul as if for a complicated, yet life saving, operation. But in this operation the patient is also the surgeon.

*And I know that if I hadn't experienced that terror of the absurd, perhaps I wouldn't have expected to love again to the heights I know. Only after accepting the loss of the world we shared, I could venture into a brave new one.*

But still the pain remains, for you still hold endless worlds in memory, which you cannot sever. A person cannot delete their memories by choice. It is only their camouflaged soul that pretends to.

*The great pretense would be not to delete those wonderful memories, but accept that I was lucky to even experience those moments, even if at times they fill me with sweet longings.*

A lovers' absurd.

*High quality problems, are they not?*

What kind of enchanted question, or perhaps a statement, is that? For such love is rare in the world, and it is most likely that every person would have chosen such a problem.

*And we have learned to see the glass as half full, be it with absurd.*

The heart's longings are merely a baby who has lost his embrace, and no enchanting thought can help in such cases.

*Then what good does the absurd do to a person?*

*Why love if ultimately everything is eliminated?*

Leave such extremes alone, for you have given in to your emotions, and you drifted as a rainbow through the range of colors, and had countless moments where such questions had no place. In other words, by true love, existential questions and anxieties are eliminated.

*Oh dear. Is this not an overly complicated ruse?*

It is a great ruse, but as all enchanted ones, here too it is only single moments of elation. For this kind of loving magics are as rare as the fabled happiness. They are expressed in impressive modesty and humility. Whenever a person conquers any peak in their dreams, they immediately return to their mundane world and the existential deliberations that are ever present, until another such loving and deceptive miracle happens.

*A shiver holds my body, for a wonderful world of thought grows in my heart.*

*Suddenly I wondered: does the loss of my love expresses my inability to perform the ruse of eliminating my existential questions, even for a few moments? Perhaps I miss those small moments when, overcomed by love, I was able to let go my hold of my existential thoughts?*

*Could it be?*

*Dear me.*

What a great compliment to lovers who have earned such a rare elation, as if they were floating in a wonderful cloud, immune from human affairs, even for a few moments. They become a facade, longings that hide the pains of the soul.

*In my imagination I thought further, that I have met the absurd and have embraced it to my soul in acceptance, as if for the first time I realized that it does not intend to disappear, and it is better that I accept that same holy burden of the absurd.*

It is truly absurd to see a person embracing one of his greatest foes, is it not?

*A loving embrace transcends any absurd.*

# How do you handle the feeling of the absurd?

# Chapter Eighteen:
## YOUR FACE IN AUTUMN

◆ ◆ ◆

How sad it is to watch your loved one's eyes, while your thoughts are concerned with his aging outer world, as a loved tree is abandoned by the leaves falling from it. For it is a gentle mirror of your future, even if in your heart you know that it will still be long before you feel such feelings.

One can also imagine that old men like me can accept the terror of others as a shared fate, but in your words you express your concern to your older loved ones, to those you have known since childhood. Can you imagine their light starting to slowly dwindle?

I look and smile into her eyes, but inside me a terrible scream rises, as if for the first time I saw the ticking clock in her heart, for I watched her absent hairs and I saw how she changed without me noticing to this day. And in that I still feel shame for not noticing when her autumn began. Then I asked myself how can a change in her appearance stir such a deep emotional turmoil in me.

How exciting it is for a person to value anew the one they love? As if discovering a great continent, whose great beauty they already know.

*Spare me tacit wisdoms, for my thoughts still dwell on my greatest fear: to forget her gentle voice.*

**See how intricate people are, as if they were the surgeons of their own souls, picking through them until they find the roots of their love...**
**Becoming so sensitive of themselves, knowing their own light and ever rising from their own darkness.**

*How much training do we need in order to know ourselves inwardly? In other words, what sensitive ear do we require to express our heart's strings against?*

**Many miss both.**

*I immediately escaped to the concerns of others as if from my own terror. I will boldly tell how extremely sensitive I am to the sounds of my loved ones' words, for a person who doesn't hear explicit love, finds its music between the lines.*

**You have now made our conversation into a bona fide operating theater.**

*What is life, if not the desire to understand?*

**What life really is?**

*I will go back to my soul, for with you one can bare oneself in distant thoughts. I had enough of experiencing myself in absence. Now I only wish to understand the root of all fears. Is that possible?*

**Do not go to such heights... One can spend a whole lifetime in describing this anxiety alone, never finding proper understanding. And what has a person left except for holding on to their crass emotions with unexplained bravery?**

*Is there another choice?*

Have you ever seen a person without any fear?

No, and you?

Seeing myself was enough to understand the distresses of those around me.

It is so pleasant to know that my thoughts are common in your world, too.

Let us return to your eyes. You have seen well the terror of your love, but were certainly sensitive enough to hide these thoughts in those moments. You could hold them in your heart.

It is terrible for a person to be helpless in front of their loved ones.

How magical is a person's ability to express endless love in their eyes, even when facing the clear terror of their loved one.

There are few wonderful people in each person's existence, to whom their heart is given to no end, as in a sacred love between the sounds of a piano and gentle thoughts.

"Many a one is unable to loosen his own chains and yet is a redeemer for his friend."[2] And how special it is to know that for a particular person you have been the greatest existential embrace in the world, one that can contain even the lake of tears in them...

And within me I knew the gentle caresses of the heart which take place in rare gazes between brave lovers, as if they could smile the great terror between them.

---

[2] Friedrich Nietzsche, *Thus Spoke Zarathustra* (Oxford: Oxford University Press, 2005) p. 50. Trans. Graham Parkes.

And even if we wonder that she might have identified in your eyes her own anxieties and valued your ability to embrace her - still, and especially for her exposure to you, you also began to fear for yourself.

*And what should a person do when a loved one contends with such challenges within him? How could he disengage himself from it and give on to the needs of the other?*

It seems that at times the greatest thing we can do for our loved ones is to simply plant in the fields of their souls the idea that we will forever serve as an intimate gaze for them, that their eyes will always have where to look.

*How cleansing is in that? What does a contending person seek if not the same familiar face?*

And it is not your opinion or your words, but your healing presence, your love.

# At extreme times, who serves for you as the most complete existential embrace? Have you told them that?

# Chapter Nineteen:
## SELF AFFIRMATION

◆ ◆ ◆

I try, and fail, to hide my thoughts from myself. Why do I fail? Because at times of elation they break out, and I can no longer repress them into other realms.

*What is the matter?*

I find around me a foreign world, and I am inside myself, observing. I go through the lives of others, to find some justification of my own world, but when I was brave enough to allow myself to express my most private emotions, I found that I wish to retire from the race common among people.

*Where is that race?*

Don't you look around you? The best of minds supply a person with existential meanings that did not stem from within them, and they pawn their lives for the aims of others

*Do these minds not express a ladle full of humanity and compassion, filling*

*and covering the dread required of a man who seeks to find the meaning of his* life? For in most cases a person is almost begging for a ready-made answer, not

being brave enough to examine the question himself.

Indeed. That is what I'm aiming at! Knowing their wisdom, I already know that it is nothing but a fiction and an obstacle to my other world, the one that seeks to create itself from within itself.

If so, now, without their help, would you be brave enough to be an island in the

sea?

I am afraid to drown in the lake of solitude, but I well know that I will discover hidden treasures in a world full of possibilities, and be a new painting in the memories of my childhood. And it is proper for a person to know their greatest dreams, and especially if they are still able to fulfill them in the challenging reality of life.

And why is it a compliment for a person to remember their unfulfilled dreams?

One must dream, even in enchanted modesty, for a person's life is nothing but small steps.

Small steps? You are asking to retire from the common race and choose your

own path.

Instead of copying the choices of others, I thought I could look into the aging eyes of strangers around the world, and discuss their thoughts with them in hidden languages. By that I will accomplish my highest passion - to be lost in the endless colorful world of existence, without holding on to the blinding background of life.

Can you accomplish such an enchanted dream?

When I looked inwards, I wondered if it is possible to live a complete life without accomplishing any dream. That thought became an abyss for my gentle soul, and I therefore decided to be brave enough to devote myself to my dreams. Even if they would end in total failure, inwardly I will at least know clearly that I tried.

There is a liberating power in that, knowing to affirm your life's choices for yourself. As if whispering to yourself silently: I would have been proud of you had I watched from the side. Despite all difficulties, you were the best you could have been. Your life is worthy.

Would your realistic dream serve as self-affirmation?

The greatest affirmation would be to accomplish my renewing dreams, as a kid who doesn't know the finality of life with its full acceptance. For I am a grown man who does not hide from reality and is aware of the finality of life…

It seems that you not only sought to realize your dreams, but that you also acknowledged your boundaries and expressed well in written form your existential passions, by which your lives will truly become significant. In your heart you have known that you could not realize all of them. You accepted that, as part of the rules of the game.

Children, at times, do not like the rules. But they will never stop playing.

# What must one experience in this world?

# Chapter Twenty:
## THE SPIRIT OF LONELINESS

◆ ◆ ◆

I woke up from a dream I couldn't cope with. In my mind's imaginations, my spirit could break the walls of its castle with conjurations that any wizard would seek. But the spirit, when alarmed, has its ways to wake itself, as if it knows its emotional abilities, and protects each person from pushing themselves beyond their possible boundaries.

From inside my world I know that the greatest nightmares have a small window of opportunity, and these nightmares come to me just before morning, as a wake up call whose noble wisdom I can't forget. In a small wonder of unclear origin, my bladder rouses me. And I wonder whether it is the nightmare that rouses me, or is it the need to relieve myself that brings about the nightmares.

As long as we do wake up. I don't like nightmares.

And still, what was there, in your dream?

Do you know that powerful whirlwind which is so common in us? That wind that expresses the limit of a person's abilities, the wind that resembles a deep pit of loneliness one cannot escape? I have seen myself running from it, as if it were coming to kill me, And I did not notice that I fell into its many traps, as if it sought me and knew my future movements from within its own decision, that every person must experience it in their lifetime. But immediately I awoke in firm resistance.

Do I know the spirit of loneliness? It meets me every day, for I am human.

Why do you not escape?

Because I have foregone the common fictions that try to coerce a person into a world where they cannot possibly experience the same human feelings, even when they are full of the terror and sadness of darkness. And human life, for the most part, is nothing but a calm lake whose water moves in gentle caress. And surprisingly, powerful winds and waves arrive, some of them drown to the depths, and some rise to a smile. In other words - I accept the rules of the format, even though I do not like them all.

Your words always seek the world of children's games, who rise after every fall, as if they knew that even a great pain comes to an end, and after it they will play and smile again.

And what should I do as an old man? I have become an expert in the game of life. A person's life is a wheel, not a triangle. They move through a rainbow of emotions, always shifting.

Well, if I consider my soul to be the best game of all, as a natural addiction of children who do not want to cease their games, I will immediately wonder, whether I would have liked to play by myself, with your image?

How would you play by yourself, with your image?

Imagine that you would have walked the world in an image other than your own, and would be exposed by chance to the story of another man, who is your world as it is expressed in our discussions...

Would you want to love him? Would you want to know you?

**Where within you do these extreme thoughts originate? A person experiences themselves better with others, and you ask the person to wonder how they are experienced by others! What do others like in them, and do they find intriguing beauty in it?**

We said one can play, so I allow myself to think whether I could find in myself a persona I would like to be near, to be sought by, to be loved by.

**How have these intimate conversations between a person and their various personas become, at times, science fiction? But if I understand you correctly, you must have sought to demand from a person that they know their own light, their beauty and sensitivity by which they are loved by others.**

I was suddenly saddened, and sought to stop this thought for I have known that people are not well-versed in the art of self-love, and therefore some would certainly abhor themselves and would say with heroic bravery that they would prefer the company of others.

Now I could see in my soul a painting of various hues taking shape in front of my eyes, portraying a whirlwind of loneliness. It is no longer a ghost chasing the person, but the lonely person trying to escape themselves, all the while knowing that this attempt is entirely hopeless.

A person becomes ghost. This is a true nightmare, an existential dread that I will escape my own soul.

It seems that our thoughts are addictive to you, and that you have found many lights and colors as if you took hold of your own hand, and together you ran long distances, with a lasting smile.

## Would you want your own love?

# Chapter Twenty-One:
## A BLIND PAINTER

♦ ♦ ♦

Thousands of people go past me, and it seems that they are all in a hurry. Where do they wish to be? How are they so certain of their way? And could it be that it is all in my imagination, could they be as lost as I am, merely seeking a way out?

**They seek solace in the uncertainty so common in reality.**

If so, how come their eyes are so bewitched that they can hide the existential dread of lacking attachment, as the vagabond who walks the streets?

**Surely some contention is better than a stupor of freedom, is it not?**

How magical it is when a person steps off the beaten track and gives in to doubt, to the nothingness in them. It is there that they find new worlds created in them.

**But who are the brave ones who blaze their own trails?**
**They must excite our soul, being able to swim in the raging water of the**

EXISTENTIAL DIALOGUES II | 97
great ocean without seeing a close island on the horizon. They walk the
dark, holding on to the candle of curiosity with which they seek to discover,
at least to an extent, themselves. And even if they learned beforehand that
during such an inquisitive journey they would encounter obstacles and
painful cuts, internally they knew that they cannot act otherwise, for by
that they would have betrayed themselves.

*It seems at times that a great pain begs for creation.*

A person's spirit recovers itself by seeking the sublime. But how can
people choose their own path?

How do you write your thoughts with me? For I do not really exist.

*And I, who bare my soul, do I exist?*

*Perhaps a common contention alongside you becomes a home of meaning to*

*me, even though I know that the ruses of my soul are nothing but an explosive*

*imagination.*

Imagine a painter standing in front of a completely empty canvas. So
empty that one can imagine the painter to be completely blind. Yet their
soul seeks to fill the canvas with colors, their soul seeks to fill his life with
meaning.

*What meaning?*

Can you not sense subtleties? Artists create out of nothing. They do not
copy the works of others. They look at the dark and find light in it, they
accept a lack of meaning just as they learn to buy more empty canvases.
But, with faith over knowledge - how well they fill them with the colors of
their spirit, with deep meaning.

*Spare me such high words! My soul is not brave enough for all of them. Is there shame in that? I am human.*

Far from shame, it is charming honesty. But you should know that in chess, even the lowly peon might decide the battle.

Therefore I do not require heights of you. Be yourself, and that is enough.

*'Be yourself, and that is enough'? Can so intimate words possibly be heard? Shall I not suddenly think that this painter could have merely looked at the empty page, as if trying to fill it with wonderful imginations but failing - and we could appreciate this attempt!*

We must embrace these efforts. For it is an achievement to walk the way of exploring meaning, even without finding it. I had never met a man who could testify that he truly found the meaning of life, but I have met many who gave up investigation and curiosity in advance by accepting the view of their surrounding.

*Is the investigation of meaning similar to love in that regard?*

It seems that it is, and many years have taught us that there is one way towards love. But the brave attempt to examine their feelings in this supreme matter as if a never ending cleansing fills them with wonder and doubt, as if they were a never ending embrace.

*But here it is an embrace one must choose anew each time.*

I constantly discover new layers in my beloved, for she has become a lake of meaning in my soul. And how would I love her if I stopped listening to the sound of her thoughts?

*I understand your curiosity for your gentle beloved, but of you? Have you had enough of yourself?*

You must ask yourself, right?

*I am famished for my passions, as a wounded animal.*

So is that painter, a lover or even a simple peon - they have all been thrown into life and are trying to create one act of meaning in their lives. Well they know in their winding consciousness that as long as their soul is full of desire, they will forever persevere in an unending yearning, like walking in an endless forest, so beautiful and intriguing that you would willingly lose yourself in it.

*And what of those who pass me by?*

*Do they all run to fill a canvas with meaning?*

They all seek to find meaning, but at times are fleeing themselves, escaping the inner voice that draws them into their dreams, and perhaps that is why their gaze turns infinitely more serious in their quick pace.

*Inwardly I wanted to express a great stop. If I could I would certainly ask them to strip bare in a nature full of green pastures, and in that great embarrassment born of exposure they would immediately shout their spirits out to the heavens. And when their veins would be full of power, they would certainly breath intimately and meet the eyes of others, those who express that human voice of contention we all share. But in this rare gaze, all masks and fictions would have disappeared from the colors of the mind suddenly lighting from within their eyes, as if from a desire that we stopped the terrible pursuit in which a person compulsively acts towards existential meanings which did* not originate from within them - for their soul's desire is a simple experience of human life.

**Look into my eyes!**

How far will we go?

**To the forests of your world.**

I am exposed to you, and suddenly you could have seen how I strive for the achievements of others, for existential meanings not my own.

Could you contend?

# What is your wish?

# Chapter Twenty-Two:
## EVIDENCE OF MEMORY

◆ ◆ ◆

Did you know that even in my old-age desires, there is still the wish for superpowers?

*You're entirely a child in your being, are you not?*

An aging child.

*What kind of superpower are we discussing?*

You would surely imagine that I would seek the heights, but my curiosity asks for even one moment of close intimacy, as knowing to the bone how others experience themselves, their struggles, their happiness.

*That is a most serious superpower!*

Imagine how intriguing is the thought that you could be understood, even once, as you imagine yourself.

*It is a rare experience in human reality, as rare as love.*

Magics of this kind happen so rarely, as that special feeling I had that I can uncensor myself to a friend. How rare is a person's ability to draw away from their collection of masks!

Then, how great is their joy when they are surrounded by uncensored loved ones who can express their souls to the extreme in the space between them, which is no less than a miracle in a person's world?

And now, from inside my world I can think of a few singular persons with whom I can take off my masks and be intimate with myself. I love them for it.

Know that their enjoyment is not less than yours, for such an exposure is a miracle and an example for them, too. They, too, long to be truly seen, without their so-beloved masks.

Is this longing not the same as the work of psychologists, who seek intimacy with their patients? And they, for their part, yearn to express their world to the bones, until their tempestuous feelings will be seen?

Moreover, the patients' yearning is even greater, for they wonder whether even after baring the fields of their souls they would still be left alone in their pain, even though they were brave, perhaps for the first time in their life, to take off their masks and express the depths of their souls to another.

And what of me?

How will I understand that I will never be able to truly meet the other, except for in short moments of elation?

I would like to declare that for such gentle moments life is worth living.

It seems that we can do nothing but accept this reality and embrace it despite its hardships.

On another tack: I ask you to consider how many wish, in moment of weakness, to exchange their problems for those of others, as if they could pick through their soul in a few moments and decide that they could handle their friends' worlds.

But it is clear to all that they have no ability to hold a different terror than the one known to them.

**They could not even bear their friends' joy.**

A person cannot even bear his own suffering at different ages.

**Are you trying to hint at something?**

There is nothing new to that! Every age brings with it amazing adventures and no less challenges. I will therefore wait patiently to come to your world.

**It seems that these days my soul seeks to experience anew your young sensations, as if yearning to feel primal excitement once again.**

But you have kept our adventurous diaries, have you not? A person carves words on paper as if on his own flesh, for the existential fear of oblivion.

**And when I read us in past days, I shiver so intensely even though I know how far my world is from those moments.**

Tricky, tricky.

In an internal dialog, very soon it is made clear that one can descend from such heights and that the mind's memories truly are the greatest superpowers *among us. For these portray short films which express the rainbow of emotions, and can express a connection between every possible hue of our private human experiences.*

And what of the struggling person?

Will he know how to find daring in being the only one in existence who can create his own memories?

Will he know how to contend with the thought that the entire rainbow of his emotions would forever be a single painting, unique in all of existence?

*Extreme questions again?*

*Teach people to live in satisfaction.*

Live in satisfaction?

When I read your life's story I remember my adventures, which were almost eliminated had I not looked again. And when I imagine my memories, I am filled with endless appreciation for existence.

*This is nothing but a blatant hint that I should continue to etch my flesh in words on the pages of the diary, to supply evidence for the court held in my soul.*

I, too, have recently bought a new diary...

# What are the most beloved memories we are afraid to forget, and what is their meaning for us?

# Chapter Twenty-Three:
## RESURRECTION

◆ ◆ ◆

In a colorful dream I walk the edge of the Earth. There, in a green landscape postcard, I see nothing but the wilderness of nature, And my gaze is full of wonder at the congregation of billions of individual details expressing a divine masterpiece. I seek to wait a moment and embrace that inner simplicity so it will not be abruptly lost on me. How can I perceive that I am only one small detail consumed by them? I close my eyes and meet the spirits of the world and I am filled with silence inside the whirlwind of my never resting thoughts. And in this miraculous moment of peace, I feel burning intensities of emotions, until, as in a volcano that has passed the threshold of power, I become brave enough to express sounds of screaming even the hidden God could not have ignored.

**I wish you could have screamed so outside of a dream sometimes, without being considered a lost mental case.**

And when I was alone in front of creation I suddenly felt so at ease, as serenity that lands in extreme moments of elation, as if I arrived by chance to a special place in the world where I could express the fibers of my being, as there was no man for whom I had to hide my inner world.

**Of these words, one can imagine that a person learns to hide his spirit throughout most journeys of his life?**

That thought is full of sadness, but I will be forced to require a deeper introspection, and express a wonder that perhaps people do not only hide essential parts of themselves from the people around them, but also from themselves.

**Where do your thoughts rush to? How can people hide from themselves?**

A baby is born into the world, and immediately its parents carve into its mind channels of thought he can no longer break free of, sometimes forever. And when its natural character seeks a place, they immediately block this budding flower with a layer of concrete - and by that a person slowly learns to adopt an acceptable outer persona by which they would be valued by others.

And were we to settle the fate of the parents' property according to the majority of cases, would it seem that in all of us there is that outside spirit which is not ours? Will we be brave enough to admit that a person has learned to love even his distant image, the one which is nothing but his self-despise?

**Such a terrible question you ask! It is obvious that its role is for our spiritual liberation.**

So many mortals express, after years of growing older, their internal absence as if it were so near them. But truly it was so hidden, so distant, so despised and alienated that, owing to all the positive reinforcements they have cultivated from the outside world throughout their lives, they were even prouder of their self-burial.

**Of these words one can imagine how dissimilar are the walking person and his inner soul.**

And what happens if that is recognized? There is so much grief for this terrible loss which is nothing but a blatant omission of life. See that person in front of you, see the wonder in their eyes, which is nothing but the birth of an adult. See how they run, as if they lost control, to the cemetery, where they embrace their inner corpse. And this love is so primal, as a close gaze of longing. This, my friend, is true resurrection!

**How much optimism there is in the idea that a person can resurrect his dead soul while still alive! A wide smile comes to my face from such an embracing psychological outlook, for in it there is hope for a brave new world.**

And after such a miraculous embrace, we will ask that the person evaluates their resurrection and affords their old world the same gaze given by a hiker who slowly comes closer to the peak of the mountain, who appreciates every step of the climb for they persist to be in motion, and if not for the struggle of their great search would most certainly never find their own grave.

But now they can look at the true colors of their soul, which were so hidden, as if they could have imagined that they were blind by choice, and has now repented and required the appropriate gaze on the rainbow of colors of their spirit - and that was some acceptance of the terrible and wonderful within them.

**And when the colors of our soul are unabashedly blatant, will we be brave enough to describe our private cemetery?**

It has some of your, and even my own, soul. For a person is nothing but the expression of their doubting conscience, many parts of which they hide well in the depths of imaginations, and its other parts they seek to the forefront of their consciousness, as if they knew that it would be the only testimony of an authentic creation coming from within them.

**See how brave is the action of a person who can sniff their way to themselves amidst the challenges of existence, which express a constant loss and search.**

Therefore these existential distances within us may somewhat shorten were we to hold the candle of longings, with which we can, little by little, light up the basements of our secrets, which have been darkened by an internal ruse of the soul, out of a defensive decree.

# Who hides there?

# Chapter Twenty-Four:
## MEANING IN LOVE.

◆ ◆ ◆

As I'm writing us, I shiver from the thought that this will be our most important conversation ever!

*Again you seed vague ideas? Speak out!*

I want to seed your heart with seeds of love you haven't known. But I'm afraid you will dismiss the lake of my thoughts by the simplicity of my words. For these already exist in your world, but you couldn't see them for the overbearing darkness.

*What do you mean?*

Towards the end of my life I feel how my thoughts seek to conclude an internal testimony, that this life was worthwhile. And as I slide into the world of my memories, I better describe the meaningful connections I had, from childhood and until damned old age.

*Did you consider me?*

Of course! First we must acknowledge that our shared soul expresses the deepest loving relationship one can have as a human being. And see how long it takes for a person to be able to express this thought to themselves without needing others as a begger does.

How is it that those internal thoughts of love break out only when you are near your end? How miserly people are with their love!

See how your words create a bloody lake of embarrassment in my cheek, after I quietly held your feelings towards me. I must admit that an abnormal emotion sought to forcefully push away my feelings directly at those peeping at the imaginations of our words, wondering whether they, too, feel love for themselves, or do they despise the vanity of our emotions.

A prophecy from within me seeks a world where the fault of love will be eliminated.

So few words describe a total cultural war, regardless of the difficulty to believe the compliments of our gentle soul, but see how hard it is to contend with the kind words of others.

Let that be. My love's words are laid in front of you as a testimony for days to come. Now I will carefully return to the gentle soil in which seeds of all kinds can be planted. But before I draw my conclusions to you, I must tell you of the seeds of love I knew through all my life with living teachers who have taught me the kinds of love common in culture. And I believed them, for what reason do they have to commit lies to my soul?

Did they lie?

It seems they did not lie, for they taught me the same wisdom they have learned themselves. But in a particular conversation with a wonderous person, we have learned by gentle spiritual exposure that the treasures of love are so common around us, when we were already entangled in numerous significant relationships.

Even in our common world we experienced more parents than is usual, and each of them was a world of meaning. It suddenly seems that it was a precious gift that you received from your mother when you were brave enough to find light in other figures. What then is the novelty of your words?

How terrible it is to express in your question the mindset which I seek to escape. For we have already learned that the greatest ill that exists is the idea that something is obvious.

Will you clarify this thought for me?

First, we discussed Plato's theory of forms, and we watched the diagram of love that has surely existed even before humans could label, organize and domesticate it to the seemingly required social order.

What is wrong with that famous longing for two loving souls to meet and love happily ever after?

Far be it, there is nothing wrong with that. But it is only a small part of the story, for it is not the only experience of love in the couple's world, but it is only a new love in their heart, as their heart loves others in greater intensities. And not only that, but their other loves do not take away from the color of their new love. On the contrary, they strengthen it.

You say that each significant relation which develops is a new color in the world, as two algorithms that create a new dimension?

Definitely! But deeper than that, and more important - see how many algorithms you have drawn around you. See how numerous are the significant relationships enveloping you even today, before that colorful true love.

But more than that, my heart holds at the same time loves for some who are no longer in my life, and even love to those who have already left this world - and this does not contradict or take away anything from my current loves. How can I contend with those emotions?

See how exciting it is for a person to look into significant emotions, which exist within them more than they could imagine. And by that their loneliness is surely smaller than they have previously thought.

You speak of a new kind of psychiatric drug, a pill one does not even need to swallow in order to be filled with intimate emotions, or alternatively - look and appreciate anew.

And even were we able to express deep loving ties to one person - then it is an endless and priceless treasure.

Is that the reason why the emotion of jealousy is so shunned? Society's attempt to domesticate love into one frame, when the human heart does not recognize these boundaries. From childhood it seeks to create meaningful and benevolent ties in its world - not only does it not recognize these boundaries, but it requires to deal with an edict it constantly violates, by loving many people of many kinds at all times.

As much is true! And what have we sought to do in this conversation except for releasing the feeling of guilt from the beating heart that does not know otherwise?

This mental embrace requires me to look inwards and deal with all of those behavioral axioms I have known from childhood, and cast doubt on all of them. For this thought of yours brings up in me extreme feelings of appreciation and gratitude to all of the wonderful people present in my world, and even now I shiver when I express to them their importance and value to me. As in creating a miracle by words, for now I walk the world with an intimate and loving sensation of meaning.

**You are not alone in the world.**

# Who is meaningful to you?

# Chapter Twenty-Five:
## ON SUICIDE

◆ ◆ ◆

I cannot understand the most important thing.

**Yourself?**

I am but a grain of sand!

**Then?**

I cannot even imagine a reason...

**Again you seek a meaning for life? I thought that question was dissolved, following our blatant thoughts and our embrace of the wisdom of the flower.**

I am no longer there. I am above it. Now my thoughts turn to struggling people,

and I cannot understand why they so desperately cling to life, even when it is

full of horrible suffering, disease and terror.

**What options do they have? The animal we call man, more than it loves life, it is addicted to it. It knows no other existence and lives its life**

suffering from immense anxiety that one day it will end, yet it is not brave enough to end its own existence. I ask, therefore: what do you offer but your complaints?

I seek to dissolve the physical suffering. I want to afford the people themselves the ability to decide their existence even before the damned diseases.

How will you do that?

One must find an acceptable way of suicide, which will be available for both the sick and the healthy, so each person who has reached their personal limit would know that they have a reasonable solution, without violence or feeling of blame.

It seems that your world sets your own private boundaries of suffering, after which you will seek to proudly end your existence. Am I close to your mind?

True. For I asked to sanctify my own life only if it is worthy of living. And when the terminal suffering meets me, I will face it and shout, with a force never seen before: Begone! I will not allow you to be a devil. I will go away only with my head raised, and not despising my own existence!

Is there a greater existential choice?

In any case, not many are so brave. And the line is not long, for it is well told that suffering cleanses a person's soul as exposed flesh caressed with iron combs. But what is that fiction? There is no purification in it, only a prolonged agony. And the end, at any rate, is the same. Then the question remains: what for?

Perhaps you meant that a suffering person can use the period of terror to properly say farewell to their loved ones? Many leave before they had the time to express their sensitive words. Or perhaps they will use the suffering of finality as if suddenly aware that it is better to finally start living? Perhaps that is the cleansing?

*Why don't schools teach a person to appreciate life before they meet at once the final terror?*

Why are you so preoccupied with suffering, being so young of age?

*For my fears to see my loved ones suffer much…*

Can you advise them to abandon your world, so long as they don't suffer?

*Existential love to the end.*

The final end.

*Wise men, such as Epicurus, have taught us that we should not be excited by the final end, for the person was 'nothing' for eons before his birth!*

And there is intellectual respite in that. But your loved ones are wholly heart, and this wisdom might not give them solace!

*Perhaps. But suffering, of course, gives even less.*

*A great love is expressed in a soul that ends itself out of strength and choice. Consider for example a loving elderly couple, who have stopped fighting the most terrible and painful thought: Who will be the first to go?*

*Boldly, they go together, as if they decided to dissolve the divine ruse and made an inspirational choice, to take responsibility themselves.*

**Is there a more authentic choice?**

Of course there isn't! And what's more, a person cannot be required to be heroic and brave. Only he can decide for himself in such fateful matters. And since it is the final end, and since it is a terminal and ultimate choice, we will have to know that a person chooses this exalted path out of a fierce and conscious thought, and not a fit of rage or sadness which might pass after an hour of existential embrace!

A person cannot choose but out of his responsibility for himself and those around him. These are therefore special, uncommon cases. But most exciting is the ability to dismiss the terror of suffering. It seems that a person slowly moves forwards towards an incredibly humane place, which seeks the intimate embrace and tries as much as it can to ease, as in a raging discussion between strictness and leniency which have been naturally decided in favor of gentleness, for we are human and conscious of the common suffering.

**And if I ask you to contend with words against ever present suffering?**

Suffering: Why do you not greet me?

Soul: Why should I greet you, when your arrival is but destruction?

Suffering: Where did you find such audacity, to be insolent of the very reason of my existence? For millenia I have been respected by others as if I restored and awakened their souls.

Soul: I have dissolved the need for your purpose, for I no longer need the common fictions, and I can explain human suffering as random, touching all without distinction, mind or purpose, as an inseparable part of life - for every person must die of something.

Suffering: the insolence! Do you not understand that some people are missing any heroic ability in their life, except for the so basic one to suffer?

Soul: I do not oppose those who find cleansing in their suffering, out of the vanity of contention, or out of religious faith. They have their place. I speak of myself. I do not need you, and as long as you assault my soul with force, I will retire in my prime, as if after a glorious victory.

Suffering: If you choose to kill yourself - is that not my own victory?

Soul: no, it is mine. For I have dissolved the question of your existence, as if you were a meaningless extra in the wonderful theater of my life, and I was brave enough to take responsibility, to my very last breath.

**How sensitive are your thoughts of that terrible suffering, and how different is your reaction. You sought to embrace the absurd, but you seek to uncompromisingly dismiss the terrible pain.**

Every masterpiece must end, and it is clear to all that the protagonist of this life-play will take responsibility for their soul in every sense imaginable.

# What is the meaning of suffering to you?

# Chapter Twenty-Six:
## THE FORGETTING OF MEMORIES

♦ ♦ ♦

**You ask to speak to me again?**

It's not like I have many options, you know...

**Well, what's on your mind?**

What could it be? Surely all those same musings I shared with you, or rather with that spirit of mine that eludes me, as one who cannot understand their excitable heart, and for this reason pushes away the object of their love.

**I understand you must draw away, but do not go too far, for I know in advance how desperate you will be to return.**

It seems that I was in an elusive trouble, for I have a fierce desire to be with you. But at the same time there is a gentle voice heard in me, seeking to draw away from the fortress of inner being, but not out of a feeling of disdain.

I invite you to disappear in distant fields, for those clarify to a person his minuteness in God's creation, his being but a grain of sand hidden from the world, and therefore meaningless.

*Even a grain of sand seeks the burning caresses of the sun.*

It wants to be the object of its love.

*And what do I want? I don't even know where to run away to, for I am rooted in you without any possibility of escaping. And how can I carry on even one day on my own, after laying bare the fields of my inner thoughts to you, as a quiet reflection asking 'what will I myself have left?'*

Why is this role-playing so attractive to you, if you cannot truly leave? What do you truly want from me?

*It seems that my most hidden desire is to know that you will be with me even were I to draw away to hidden places where your entry is forbidden.*

But if you will be there without me, who will you be?

*That is the crux of the matter, the existential fear that all of our shared words would disappear as if they never were, by the damned crimes of forgetfulness.*

Is that why you sometimes draw away from your own mind? To discover, upon returning, that I am still here, safeguarding your thoughts?

*I am brave enough for many wars, but the loss of our private thoughts is the highest terror in existence for me.*

There is no solace for such helplessness, but it would be a great compliment to cherish the deep relationship in our spirit now, as if it were a testimony of the dark days we spent.

*We were a small light, but we were.*

And in old age you know that I could have surpassed you, and, with a wave of my hand, eliminate part of the difficult memories we share, for not every truth should be known.

*And were you not the doorkeeper, could we have had the same intimate relationship? In that case I would have most likely run away from you.*

But this is a very common psychological reality, and in it, too, there is a lot of power, as a cry of elation in moments of danger.

*Suddenly it seems that perhaps all of our conversations are nothing but a sophisticated ruse you have created to deal with the terror of forgotten memories.*

It is but you. Only you remember from within you, only you forget from within you, only you escape from within you, only you beg for your return, only you love yourself.

*Do I speak to myself, then, rather than hearing voices?*

You never speak enough.

*I heard that!*

# What do we think of the voices coming from within us?

# Chapter Twenty–Seven:
## LIFE IN THE ABSENCE OF SELF

◆ ◆ ◆

An older woman walks in a central avenue, her eyes full of tears and she ceaselessly squeals at the people: "I never had the chance to be me". That event was so brazen to my feelings.

**How can you spend a whole life in absence?**

Not only that, but by shouting she expressed two similar apprehensions: one, that she did not have the opportunity and that the freedom of choice was taken from her, and two, that she knew the desired soul, her ideal "I", but throughout her life, had somehow missed it.

**And if she weren't herself, who were she really?**

That is an insensitive question. Please come closer to one who contends. She was certainly a complete and wonderful person even in her absence.

**How can a person express in public the great terror from within them, as if feeling to the bone that the end were near, and that perhaps they could no longer change their life's conclusion?**

*Stop expressing wars in her gentle spirit, for she was wholly a wonderful honesty.*

Her words are hard as they are touching, for they are common among all of us. Her words are wonderful because they hide in our souls. Her blatant anxiety is nothing but courage.

*Then, perhaps she is yelling to the crowds in order to save them, as if to say the brazen truth directly to their eyes, with no possibility of escape, and be in her feelings to the point of healing terror?*

Painfully healing. For a person is not born an expert in living, and there is no guide for existence but those who seek that he would be like them. And if so, she screams her soul-shaking words to the public, as if begging to watch again the existential questions, lest others come to her terrible end conclusion.

*How can a person know what to ask?*

First, they would be aware that they have never asked anything, and up until now only adopted the fictions of others - and with this conclusion and understanding would have already gained much.

And when they have been brave enough to gaze at this terrible truth, they would certainly project their own life's story on their choices, or more precisely - their own absence - for they have chosen only by the force of others, and never truly from within themselves.

And if they would be brave enough to still choose to live when this discovery had been made, it is a sign that for the first time they realized that they were not truly alive before it, that they had, in fact, missed so many years pleasing the whole world but themselves - then they would certainly continue to wonder on the most miraculous question a person can ask.

*Teach me questions.*

Don't you understand? She demands that the people ask questions as if they were alone in the world, as if they were the first who have ever asked about existence.

She demands that the person asks what is the meaning of life, and no one can answer but that person himself.

She demands that people ask about their most secret desires, and no one can answer but they themselves.

She demands that people ask what Is the meaning of suffering, and no one can answer but they themselves.

She demands that people ask so they can make their own mistakes, so their mistakes would not be the fictions of others.

She demands that people question and doubt everything, in order to draw their own portrait, even if scratched and scarred.

*I immediately sought to embrace her so much.*

Embrace her with your existential questions, and she would be happy inside.

*But what would happen were I to ask these deep questions and lack appropriate answers? Why should I fill myself with such high anxiety? For it is a great comfort for a person to shelter under the wings of others, and remove responsibility from their world.*

Are you not sensitive to subtleties? That exactly expresses her deepest pain, for she has hidden in others' choices for her and assimilated into them, and when she came to the finish line she decided that it was all in vain. Can you fathom such a self loss of life?

Then a person is capable of inner suicide when he expresses his choice not to choose, by giving in to the choices of others, as if he feels safe in them - but this is also necessarily a choice!

A choice perhaps, but deep down it is nothing but escape.

As much as the person can avoid their own soul in different guises, ultimately an inner voice screams from within them and seeks the desired honesty for their deep questions, the ones they were able to brazenly hide from themselves as in an inexplicably intricate game of repression. And when they burst through the inner walls in the form of that screaming woman, they can no longer be avoided, for she stands there with her soul-shaking words.

And now they can do nothing but face themselves as if they put a mirror in front of their colorful eyes and look as deeply and inescapably as they can into their spirit. In this moment of terror they would wonder, internally, on the coming finality of life, and ask how much choice did they have in their world? Then, for the first time in their world, they would be brave enough for their great questions, and, with the obvious concerns of contention, would at the same time feel that they have become something they have never been in common reality - become themselves.

# Did you ask the same questions?

# Have you truly been yourself as if you were alone in the world?

# My sources of inspiration

Albert Camus - The Myth of Sisyphus

Viktor E. Frankl -  Man's Search for Meaning

Fyodor Dostoevsky - The Karamazov Brothers

Friedrich Nietzsche -  Thus Spoke Zarathustra

Leo Tolstoy - The Death of Ivan Ilyich

I would kindly ask you to express your sincere thoughts and write a review on my Amazon book page (:

You can also contact me here:

Daniel.chechick@gmail.com

IG: chechick.daniel

Printed in Great Britain
by Amazon

49831407R00078